SAVE MY 401(k)!

What You Can Do NOW
to Rebuild Your Retirement Future

DAVID RYE

Mc Graw Hill

New York   Chicago   San Francisco   Lisbon   London   Madrid   Mexico City
Milan   New Delhi   San Juan   Seoul   Singapore   Sydney   Toronto

Library of Congress Cataloging-in-Publication Data

Rye, David E.
    Save my 401(k)! : what you can do now to rebuild your retirement future / David
Rye.
        p.   cm.
    Includes index.
    ISBN 978-0-07-173631-2
      1. 401(k) plans.   2. Individual retirement accounts—United
States.   3. Retirement—Planning—United States.   I. Title.

    HD7105.4.R94   2010
    332.024'0145—dc22   2009052621

1 2 3 4 5 6 7 8 9 10 11 12 13 14 15 16 DOC/DOC 1 9 8 7 6 5 4 3 2 1 0

ISBN 978-0-07-173631-2
MHID   0-07-173631-X

McGraw-Hill books are available at special quantity discounts to use as premiums and
sales promotions or for use in corporate training programs. To contact a representative,
please e-mail us at bulksales@mcgraw-hill.com.

This publication is designed to provide accurate and authoritative information in regard
to the subject matter covered. It is sold with the understanding that the publisher is
not engaged in rendering legal, accounting, securities trading, or other professional
services. If legal advice or other expert assistance is required, the services of a
competent professional person should be sought.
      *—From a Declaration of Principles Jointly Adopted by a Committee of the
American Bar Association and a Committee of Publishers and Associations*

Contents

Preface

IF YOU ARE one of the millions of Americans counting on your 401(k) to help you retire comfortably, then you're probably disappointed in what has happened to its value over the past few years. To compound your retirement problems, traditional fixed pensions are fast disappearing, and many employers have stopped matching their employees' 401(k) contributions. On top of that, the "great recession" that started in 2008 has had a devastating effect on the economy. The resulting market meltdown has tarnished everyone's concept of what it takes to make good investment decisions. Many of us simply choose to sit on the sidelines and painfully watch as our 401(k) holdings continue to shrink in value. What can you do to save your 401(k)?

For starters, you've got to play an active role in managing your 401(k) plan because if you do nothing but watch from the sidelines, you will lose even more. Although taking on that responsibility may seem like a daunting task, it doesn't have to be. Managing your 401(k) can be challenging, but if you let it, it can also be fun and financially rewarding beyond your wildest expectations. *Save My 401(k)!* shows you how to do that in these tough economic times.

As you read this practical book, you will discover how to circumvent your 401(k) problems and how to immediately start making sound investment decisions that are right for you. You'll also learn how to substantially reduce the risk you've been exposed to in the past. Each chapter includes strategies that build on what you've learned from previous chapters. You can select the approaches that are best for you, based upon your own situation. This book has four distinct parts. In Part 1 you'll get a better understanding of what's in your 401(k) and the investment options available to you. Part 2 shows how to find the money you'll need to make sound investments in stock, bond, and index funds. Part 3 addresses preretirement steps for you to consider. Putting together everything you've learned is the theme of Part 4.

There's also a rich array of "here's why it works" illustrations throughout the book. Many illustrations are supplemented with related websites for additional information should you need it.

The sooner you start actively managing your 401(k), the sooner you'll see its value heading up rather than down. *Save My 401(k)!* contains all the elements you'll need to improve your current and future financial position.

Acknowledgments

WITHOUT THE HELP of my literary agent, Michael Snell, this book would never have been written. He worked with the publisher, prompted me, and, more important, motivated me to push for the assignment. For all of his help I am extremely grateful.

Thanks also to my friend and associate, Pam Selthun, who helped me with the many details of manuscript preparation in order to meet a tough delivery deadline. A special thanks goes to Kristi and Kori, my daughters, who put up with me and my grouchy moods after numerous late nights working on the final manuscript. If it had not been for their inspiration, I never would have completed this book.

PART 1

UNDERSTANDING YOUR PLAN

The wait-and-hope syndrome is one reason why many Americans are antsy about what's happening to their 401(k) plans. *Money* magazine recently published an article expounding on the fact that most 401(k) owners don't even know what they own, let alone know what their plans' investment options are. Many don't select investments in any sort of systematic way. It's no wonder that their portfolios are about as healthy as a bucket of fried chicken.

Saving your hard-earned money in a 401(k) is one of the smartest investment decisions you'll ever make. These plans offer significant tax breaks and numerous other advantages, with very few drawbacks. But if you want to get the full benefit of your plan, then you have to know what's in it, how it works, how to evaluate the available investment options, and how to manage your plan to optimize your retirement benefits.

CHAPTER 1

Getting to Know Your 401(k)

DO YOU EVER wake up at night worried about the financial setbacks you're having with your 401(k) plan in this chaotic economy? Does it aggravate you when your plan's value seems to be going in the wrong direction—down? The stock market nosedive shown in Figure 1.1 on the following page came on the heels of the 2008 recession and devastated many 401(k) plans. The figure shows what happened to the average price of a stock on the New York and NASDQ Stock Exchanges from March 2008 through March 2009.

Many investors had made what they thought were good investments only to see a significant drop in the value of their accounts in 2008 and well into 2009. Some blamed the 401(k) itself, but that's like shooting the messenger

FIGURE 1.1 ◆ Average price of a U.S. stock (March 2008–March 2009)

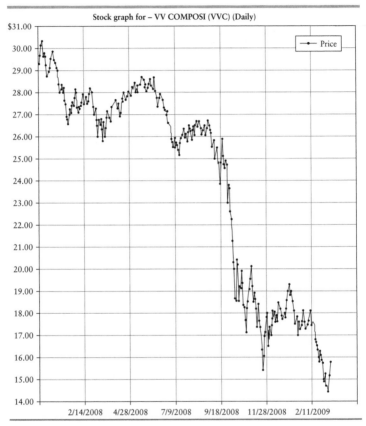

Source: *Vectorvest.com*

who brings bad news. If you're willing to take the time to really get to know what's inside your 401(k), then you can start growing it into a nest egg that will help you retire comfortably.

How 401(k)s Work

Employer-sponsored 401(k) plans are retirement savings plans that were created by the Internal Revenue Service (IRS) in 1978. They allow you to put some of your income away now to use later when you need it for retirement. To motivate people to start saving in their 401(k) plans, the federal government, in its infinite wisdom, created tax breaks for participants.

The plans rapidly grew in popularity when employees discovered that the plans allowed their employers to make tax-sheltered contributions directly into their 401(k) accounts. In addition, they liked that 401(k) plans were more portable than traditional pension plans because they could easily be moved from one employer to the next. Employers also liked 401(k)s because they were less expensive to fund than defined-benefit retirement plans and easier to administer.

When you elect to participate in your employer's 401(k) program, you must agree to deposit into the plan some amount of money from your paycheck. You determine the amount to be deposited. Some employers match all or part of your contributions. You don't pay federal income tax on contributions until you withdraw your money. What your 401(k) will be worth when you retire depends on three basic factors: how much you and your employer contributed into the plan, what rate of return you realized from the investments you made, and the length of time your money remained in the plan before you withdrew it.

The Employee Retirement Income Security Act (ERISA) is the federal law that sets the standards for employee retirement plans, including 401(k)s. Employers are required to provide to their employees documentation that describes the daily operation and benefits of their 401(k) plan, identifies the trust fund that holds their employees' accounts, and keeps them up-to-date on their account balance, deposits, and earnings.

The Economy and Your Future

Now that the first decade of the twenty-first century is over, what's in store for the second decade and how will it affect your retirement? For one thing, we've all inherited a mountain of private and public debt. Consumer spending will no longer get a steroidal fix from cheap loans and cashed-out home equity. Lending terms will be significantly tougher for both individuals and businesses alike.

Global competition will be fierce in manufacturing and services, keeping a lid on U.S. wages. The mountain of government debt incurring will inevitably result in higher inflation, more taxes, and higher interest rates. Foreign creditors such as China will keep lending us money, but they'll demand a premium price for their loans. All of these economic events will dampen corporate profits, restrain stock prices, and hamper employers' ability to match employee 401(k) contributions.

The good news is that on average we'll live twenty years longer than our parents. Unfortunately, that puts more pressure on retirement accounts. If you plan to retire in your sixties or earlier, you could live thirty or more years in retirement. So it's never too early or late to plan for a retirement that may last longer than your working career.

The age you retire is up to you, regardless of your income level. The security of your retirement will depend on focusing your attention on your financial goals. Your 401(k) plan is more important now than it ever was. Fortunately, the laws affecting 401(k) plans make it easier for Americans to save, but they also make workers more responsible for their own retirements.

What's in Your Plan?

Your 401(k) plan is a tax-deferred savings account similar to an Individual Retirement Account (IRA) with several important exceptions. Your employer owns your 401(k) plan, which is an important distinction you need to understand. All employees are allowed to participate in their company's plan. The money that you contribute into your part of the 401(k) plan belongs to you, and any contribution that your employer makes on your behalf belongs to you once you've satisfied vesting conditions set by your employer.

Tax-exempt contributions to your 401(k) come directly from your paycheck up to $15,500, $22,000 if you're 50 or older, each year. You can contribute to your 401(k) plan only while you're still working for the employer that set it up. If you change employers and your new employer doesn't have a 401(k) plan, you can convert it to an IRA. If your new employer has a 401(k) plan, you can transfer it over into your new employer's plan.

Some employers contribute to their employees' 401(k) plans as their way of encouraging their workers to participate in their retirement plan. Employers choose the amount they're willing to contribute as part of a profit-sharing program or routinely make matching contributions that have nothing to do with the company's profit. Matching contributions are made at a specified percentage of each employee's contribution. In some cases, employees are not 100 percent vested in matching contributions until they have been in the program for a specified period of time. However, more and more employers are offering safe-harbor 401(k) plans, which make their contributions 100 percent vested (i.e., the money is yours) when they are made. Your own contributions are always 100 percent vested.

An employer's contribution is one of the most valuable features of a 401(k) because it's like getting free money deposited into your retirement savings account. Employers choose their own schedule for depositing money into your account. They may do it every payday or on a monthly, quarterly, or annual basis. In some plans, you get their contribution only if you match it. Employers are not required by federal law to make contributions, and many stopped doing so when the recession hurt their businesses.

You typically have to work for a specified length of time, such as three or six months, before you can leave the company without forfeiting your employer's contribution. Make sure you know what the time requirements are in your plan. Your employer's contribution gives you an incentive to save, and it gives your account a powerful boost to grow through the appreciation of the investment choices you make. It therefore makes sense for you to always contribute at least the full amount that your employer will match. Most employees are allowed to participate in their employer's 401(k) if they are at least twenty-one years old and have been with the company thirty to ninety days. The employer match feature might not start until you have been with the company for a longer period of time.

The rules that govern your employer's 401(k) plan are spelled out in a Summary Plan Description (SPD) available from your human resources department. It outlines eligibility requirements, how to contribute, and how to withdraw money. Make sure you know the answers to these questions about the important features of your 401(k):

◆ Does your employer offer matching contributions, and if so, when are they made and what are the vesting requirements?

- What are the minimum and maximum amounts you are allowed to contribute?
- When are you eligible to participate in your 401(k) plan?
- What investment choices do you have, and how do you change an investment choice after you've made it?
- If you quit your job, are you allowed to leave your money in the plan?
- What administrative expense fees do you pay? Are there any other special fees that you may have to pay?
- Whom can you talk to if you need advice? How do you contact them? What are the function and responsibility of each contact person you're given?
- How can you get an itemized statement of your account whenever you want it? Is it available online?

401(k) Advantages and Disadvantages

One of the immediate advantages of a 401(k) plan is that once you start participating in one, it instantly reduces your current taxable income. You don't have to pay federal income tax on the money that is contributed into your plan until you withdraw it. Here's an example of how you save on federal income taxes when you participate in a 401(k) assuming the following:

- ◆ Your monthly gross pay is $5,000.
- ◆ You are in the 27 percent federal income tax bracket.
- ◆ Social Security and Medicare (FICA/FUTA) taxes are 7 percent.
- ◆ You are allowed to contribute up to 10 percent of your gross pay into a 401(k), which is $500 per month for this example.

Table 1.1 shows what your take-home pay would be if you chose not to participate in the 401(k) versus what it would be if you did participate.

In this example, had you contributed $500 to your retirement plan, you would have reduced your take-home pay by only $150. Without the 401(k), taxes eat away the money you could have been saving. And, we did not count

TABLE 1.1 ◆ Tax savings comparison between not participating and participating in a 401(k)

Payroll Categories	Nonparticipating Employee	Participating Employee
Gross pay	$5,000	$5,000
Retirement contribution	$0	$500
Federal income tax	$1,350	$1,000
FICA/FUTA taxes	$350	$350
Take-home pay	$3,300	$3,150

the potential investment earning (i.e., interest) you would have made on your $500 contribution.

If you are participating in an employer-matching 401(k) plan, make sure you know how much you have to contribute to get 100 percent of the matching funds. For example, let's say you earn $50,000 and are allowed to contribute 6 percent of your salary ($3,000) into your 401(k). Your employer has agreed to match 50 percent of every employee's contribution, or in your case $1,500. You end up with $4,500 in your account after contributing only $3,000 of your own money. You also need to know the maximum amount you're allowed to contribute into your 401(k). If you're 50 or older, you may be allowed to contribute more using what Uncle Sam calls a "catch-up" option.

While the tax advantages you get with a 401(k) are great, watch out for the flip side of the coin. If you think that since the money in your plan is yours that you can get at it whenever you want, watch out! There are strict rules that dictate when you can withdraw money without having to pay a penalty.

Many companies permit you to make hardship withdrawals for specified reasons. If you're able to qualify for a hardship withdrawal and under age 59½, you will be required to pay federal, state, and local taxes if applicable, and you may be required to pay a 10 percent early withdrawal penalty. Hardship withdrawals are only permitted if you can show you have an immediate financial need and can prove to your employer that you have exhausted all other financial resources to get the money you need. The hardship situations that have the IRS stamp of approval are:

- payment of post-secondary education-related expenses for you, your spouse, dependent children, and nondependent children
- costs related to the purchase of your primary residence or to prevent an eviction from your primary residence, such as a foreclosure
- medical expenses not covered by insurance for you, your spouse, dependent children, and nondependent children

You can withdraw only the amount you need to meet your hardship situation. The amount of money you're allowed to withdraw must come from the money you've contributed. It cannot include money from investment returns or employer contributions. If your plan allows you to borrow money, you may be required to take a loan before taking a hardship withdrawal. You will have to repay the loan and interest with after-tax dollars. In some cases, the interest you pay goes back into your 401(k) account balance. Check your plan to see if it allows you to do this.

Rolling Over Retirement Accounts

Transferring your money from one tax-deferred retirement account such as a 401(k) into another is known as a rollover, or a trustee-to-trustee transfer. There may come a time when it makes sense to roll over your 401(k) into a new retirement plan. For example, if you quit your job and start working for another employer who has its own 401(k) plan, then you may want to roll over your old 401(k) into the new plan. If the new employer doesn't have a plan, you can move your 401(k) into your own IRA or you can leave it with your old employer—if that is allowed. In some cases, your old employer will allow you to leave your money in their plan even after you quit working for them. If you are dissatisfied for whatever reason with your current plan, you may roll it over into another plan such as an IRA, as described next.

If you choose to transfer your money, you can do it by using either a direct transfer or a sixty-day rollover process. A direct transfer is the best choice because your money is transferred directly from the old trustee to the new trustee into your tax-deferred account. If you elect to use a sixty-day rollover transfer, you are given a check for the amount that's in your account from the old trustee and have sixty days to deposit the money with your new trustee.

You are allowed to do only one rollover of the same account once a year. If you miss the sixty-day deadline or are not able to deposit the full amount that you withdrew, you will owe tax on the amount not transferred plus a penalty if you're under age 59½. Therefore, pay close attention to the paperwork involved in moving money between retirement accounts. The IRS website (irs.gov) has easy-to-understand guidance on transfers.

Some employers prefer to give you a check for your 401(k) balance. If they do, have them make the check out to the financial institution (i.e., trustee) that administers the account where you want the money to go. If the check is made out to you, the employer is required to withhold 20 percent of your account value as federal withholding taxes. You'll then have to file a special form with the Internal Revenue Service (IRS) to get that money back. The IRS will return the withheld taxes when you provide them with confirming documentation that you transferred your old account into another tax-deferred account. You don't want to go through this IRS exercise; use the direct transfer option.

Replacing a 401(k) with an IRA

Individual retirement accounts, or IRAs as they are universally called, offer special tax breaks when used to save for retirement. They're like your 401(k) plan, but with IRAs you have access to an almost limitless number of investment options to choose from that aren't available in 401(k) plans. Even if your employer has a 401(k) plan, you can open an IRA yourself. Individual retirement accounts are separate from your 401(k) and have limits on the amount you can contribute each year. Depending on your income and whether you have a retirement plan at work, you might be able to deduct the amount you deposit in an IRA on your tax return if you meet certain income restrictions, as outlined in Table 1.2. Consult IRS Publication 590 at irs.gov for specific IRA rules and questions.

If you're married, each spouse can have his or her own IRA and make contributions if at least one spouse had taxable income in the year in which the contributions were made. Both spouses can contribute separately up to the IRA limit. Contributions can be made throughout the tax year and up until the April 15 tax deadline. If one spouse

TABLE 1.2 ♦ **IRA deduction schedule effective 2010**

Filing Status	Adjusted Gross Income (AGI) Limits	Amount of Deduction
Single or head of household and you are covered by a retirement plan at work	$53,000 or less $53,001 to $63,000 $63,001 or more	Full deduction Partial deduction No deduction
Married filing jointly and spouse has a retirement plan at work	$159,000 or less $159,001 to $169,000 $169,001 or more	Full deduction Partial deduction No deduction
Single or head of household and you are NOT covered by a retirement plan at work	Any amount	Full deduction
Married filing jointly and spouse DOES NOT have a retirement plan at work	Any amount	Full deduction

has more than one IRA account, the annual contribution limit applies to all the IRA accounts. There are penalties if the annual contribution limit is exceeded.

Contributions to an IRA are a do-it-or-lose-it proposition. If you don't make a contribution in a given year, you can't make it up in the following tax year. You're allowed to contribute up to $5,000 a year or $6,000 a year if you are 50 or older. You can deduct your IRA contribution if you meet certain income restrictions that are covered in Table 1.2. The income limits are based on the amount of your adjusted gross income (AGI), which is the sum of your work income plus any other income you had such as interest and dividends from investments.

You can withdraw money from your IRA any time you want, but the IRS will apply a 10 percent penalty on unqualified withdrawals. You are allowed to take qualified withdrawals without penalty if you are 59½ or older, are disabled, use your withdrawal to pay for college or other qualified educational expense, or withdraw up to $10,000 to pay for a first-time home purchase. All or a portion of withdrawals are taxed at your income tax rate in the year you took the withdrawal. You must begin to take withdrawals following the year you turn 70½.

Contributing into your IRA even when it's not deductible on your tax return is still a good idea. Your contributions will continue to help grow your retirement finances, and your investment growth is still tax deferred until you withdraw the money. The nondeductible amount you contribute to your IRA is called your "IRA Basis," which you will want to record. Since you've already paid taxes on that money, it's not taxed when you withdraw it from your IRA.

Up to this point, our discussion has been limited to traditional IRAs. Another type of IRA worthy of your consideration is the Roth IRA. It was named after Senator William Roth, who sponsored it. Unlike traditional IRAs, Roth IRA withdrawals are tax free in part because Roth IRA deposits are not tax deductible. However, your investments inside the account continue to grow tax free. And, you don't have to start making withdrawals from a Roth IRA when you reach 70½ as is the case with traditional IRAs. You're eligible to participate in a Roth IRA if your AGI falls within the ranges shown in Table 1.3. Consult IRS Publication 590 at irs.gov for specific IRA rules and questions.

TABLE 1.3 ◆ Roth IRA participation schedule effective 2010

Filing Status	Adjusted Gross Income (AGI) Limits	Amount of Deduction
Married filing jointly or head of household	Up to $159,000 $159,001 to $169,000	Full deduction Declining deduction
Single	Up to $101,000 $101,001 to $116,000	Full deduction Declining deduction
Married filing separately	Up to $100,000	Declining deduction

The IRS penalties are steep if you contribute to a Roth when the rules prohibit it. You are allowed to convert money from a traditional IRA to a Roth IRA. You'll have to pay taxes on the money you use for the conversion because all Roth contributions must be made with after-tax dollars. If you believe that your tax bracket will be at least as high when you retire as it was while you were working and you want to defer withdrawals past age 70½, then a Roth may be right for you. You're also allowed to make tax-free withdrawals from a Roth at any time after you have held it for at least five years.

You can open a traditional IRA or Roth IRA at most financial institutions and banks that sell investment vehicles such as mutual funds and bank savings accounts. The institution you choose should depend on how well the investment options they offer fit into your retirement plan. Whatever institution you choose will act as the trustee for your IRA. Most trustees charge an annual fee (usually less than $100) to maintain your account. This fee may be waived once your IRA reaches a certain dollar amount. When you open an IRA account, the trustee will give you an IRA adoption agreement that describes the operational details of your account, the types of allowable investments, contribution limits, and the process for making deposits and withdrawals. Your account is opened when you sign the adoption agreement.

One big advantage an IRA has over a 401(k) plan is that you can pick almost any investment for your account. You're not limited to the investment list your employer has selected for its 401(k) plan. This extra control over your investment options is a powerful way to grow your retirement account. Common IRA investment options, which will be discussed in Chapter 2, are certificates of deposit (CDs), money market funds, mutual funds, stocks, and bonds.

Some people like to open several IRA accounts—one for mutual funds, one for stocks, one for CDs, and so on, which can get confusing. Most brokerage firms, such as Fidelity Investments and Charles Schwab, can consolidate your separate investments into one IRA account to simplify the task of managing your investments. There are several reasons why you might want to convert your 401(k) into an IRA:

- An IRA can be a great substitute if your 401(k) investment lineup is not performing well. And, if your employer is not contributing to your plan, switching may be a no-brainer.
- You're stuck with whatever investment options your employer has deemed are best for you. With an IRA, you're free to choose the investment options that you know are best for you.
- An IRA has the same tax advantages as a 401(k) in that as long as your money stays in the account, there's no need to worry about taxes.
- If you invest in a Roth IRA, you don't have to worry about whether taxes will skyrocket because you won't owe taxes on the money when it's withdrawn.

- An IRA offers generous deadlines to make your contributions. The IRS gives you 15½ months to invest in an IRA. For example, the 2010 tax year contribution window extends from January 1, 2010, until April 15, 2011.
- An IRA promotes disciplined savings. You can instruct the financial institution that holds your account to automatically withdraw a specified amount of money on a certain date every month from your checking or savings account. Autopilot savings is an excellent way to grow wealthy.

Applying What You've Learned

- Tax-sheltered accounts such as 401(k) plans and IRAs are powerful tools you can use to help build your retirement funds.
- It is well worth your time to adjust your 401(k) contribution to qualify for your employer's maximum matching contribution.
- A trustee-to-trustee direct transfer is by far the easiest and least risky way to handle the rollover process. You have sixty days to exercise a sixty-day rollover to avoid penalties and tax consequences.
- Check your 401(k) Plan Prospectus and Summary Plan Description for answers to most of the

questions you might have. Contact your plan's trustee for advice and consultation.

♦ You must start making withdrawals from traditional IRAs (Roth IRAs excluded) at age 70½. Tax-free withdrawals from Roth IRAs can be made after they have been held for five years. Withdrawals from traditional IRAs can be made without incurring a penalty after you reach age 59½.

♦ The rules change every year for 401(k) and IRA plans, so consult IRS Publication 590 at least annually. It's available online at irs.gov. Annual IRA contribution limits apply to all your IRA accounts combined.

CHAPTER 2

Investment Options

DO YOU KNOW what investment options you have in your 401(k) plan? The pat answer of "mutual funds and bonds" won't cut it. If someone took a peek at all the stuff you've got crammed into your 401(k), would it look as cluttered as your old high school gym locker? Or worst yet, is all of your money sitting in just one untouched investment that isn't growing? If you want to save your 401(k), you've got to know by name each of the investment options that are available to you and how they have performed for at least the past two years.

What Are Your Options?

When an employer sets up a 401(k) plan, it provides employees with a menu of investment options. The employer also selects an investment broker such as Fidelity Investments or TD Ameritrade to administer the plan. Your plan's provider sends investors accounting statements and often provides online access to individual accounts.

The money in your 401(k) account is invested according to the choices you make from the menu of available options in your plan. Since your employer wants to make it relatively easy for you to review and choose from these investment options, most plans offer a website that fully explains each option.

Don't let fluctuations in your account balance discourage you from regularly contributing. Your share prices will increase and decrease on a daily basis. When share prices are down, your contribution buys more shares. When share prices are up, your contribution buys fewer shares. Over time, your cost per share will average out, a concept called dollar cost averaging.

Option Fees

When the cost of gas goes up another dime, most of us take notice. The gas stations are so aware of their shoppers' sensitivity that most post signs displaying today's gas prices. But, you can't get upset about the price you're paying if you don't know what you're paying.

The investment options that your 401(k) plan provides are not free. You're charged various fees for the management of each investment option you select. These charges are not unusual; they're in all 401(k) plans. But you need to know what fees you're paying and whether they are reasonable. Determining if you are paying a reasonable amount can be a challenge because you won't get an invoice that lists exactly what you're paying. In most cases, fees are deducted from your investment returns and will ultimately reduce your eventual balance. Ask your provider to give you a list of all fees authorized by your employer to charge to your 401(k) plan.

Here's why it is important to know what fees you are paying. Let's say you and your friend work for different companies and each of you have contributed $5,000 annually into your respective 401(k) plans over the next thirty-five years. You both earn an average of 8 percent on your respective investments over that time frame. Your plan charges 1 percent annually while your friend's plan charges 2 percent. Is a lousy percentage point a big deal? At the end of the thirty-five years, you will have earned $641,000 while your friend will have earned $521,000.

As you can see, paying just 1 percent more in annual fees is a big deal, since you made $120,000 more than your friend. Excessive fees can cost you as much as 20 percent of your account's value. So, it pays to know what your plan charges.

Where Funds Fit In

Every 401(k) plan comes loaded with a variety of actively and passively managed fund options. Some plans will allow you to invest in individual stocks. All plans offer safe places to invest your cash like money market funds and certificates of deposit (CDs). Mutual funds are pooled investments that are professionally managed and offer diversified investment options. They're popular with people who are not interested in picking individual stocks and bonds. The fund's managers do that for you either on an active or passive management basis. Actively managed funds employ managers who are constantly evaluating the market and selecting investments they believe should perform better than others.

Passively managed funds follow the logic that it's unlikely active fund managers will beat the market over the long term. Therefore, passively managed funds seek simply to match the performance of the market over the short term and long term by buying investments that replicate a particular market's index. You pay a higher fee for actively managed funds than you do for passively managed funds.

Exchange traded funds (ETFs) are passively managed funds. They are typically made up of a market basket of securities (i.e., a mixture of different securities) and are traded like stocks on the market exchanges, such as the New York Stock Exchange. As investors fled the recession-ravaged actively managed fund market in 2008, the investments in ETFs increased dramatically. They offered instant diversification, representing a section of the market in a single security, and, like a stock, investors could buy or sell an ETF at any time. Gold and other metal-based ETFs are popular inflation hedges.

Many mutual fund companies, irritated by the increasing popularity of index funds, have added ETFs to their lineup of regular funds. Some funds have exorbitant management fees, so look for index funds with the lowest expense ratio. You can find them at the major fund houses like Vanguard, T. Rowe Price, Fidelity Investments, and Charles Schwab.

A number of firms, including Fidelity and Vanguard, have created target retirement funds that automatically rebalance at regular intervals. These funds have different asset allocations that depend on your target retirement date. As you get closer to your retirement age, these funds typically become more conservative in how they balance their assets.

Option Categories

Recent studies show that the primary reason for the dismal 401(k) returns of the past was that participants paid little attention to the investment options available to them. For example, many participants didn't have enough money in premium stock mutual funds, which historically have higher returns than other investment options. Those in their twenties only invested about 50 percent of their accounts in stock mutual funds. That is low for young investors who may not retire for forty or more years. Many of those in their thirties and forties were too timid with their stock allocation. What the percentages in the study didn't show is the number of 401(k) participants who have most of their savings in their plan's money market fund. At this level, when money market funds are only paying 2 to 3 percent, they'll be lucky to break even with the rate of inflation.

It doesn't matter how young or old you are. You could be on the verge of retirement and still should invest in a mix of assets that will provide you with a decent rate of return. Why? Life fortunately doesn't stop after you leave the company's retirement party. You could still have thirty or more years of the good life ahead of you—if you can afford it. If your 401(k) is just creeping along, it will get devoured by the inflation demon.

Cash options are generally insured by the Federal Deposit Insurance Corporation (FDIC). The FDIC's coverage includes principal and interest through the date of the bank failure up to the applicable insurance limit for each deposit. If a bank closes, interest ceases on all accounts. If another bank acquires the deposits from the failed bank, the acquiring bank becomes responsible for reestablishing interest rates and beginning the accrual of interest after the date of the bank failure. The acquiring bank may change the interest rate on the acquired deposits, but depositors may withdraw their insured funds without penalty if they choose to do so. If no acquiring bank is found for the deposits, the FDIC pays the depositors directly for their insured amounts. You have the right to cash in your CD without penalty.

Following are six investment options to consider. Each is made up of subcategories. For example, the domestic stock fund category has three subcategories: domestic stocks, international stocks, and a mix of domestic and international stocks.

- **Cash.** Money market funds (MMFs) are saving accounts that pay a higher interest rate than passbook savings accounts and are usually insured. You can move your money into and out of a MMF at any time without paying a penalty. Some retirement plans allow you to save your money in CDs, which earn more interest than savings and money market accounts. However, unlike savings and money market accounts, you can't withdraw money from a CD until its specified maturity date unless you pay an early withdrawal penalty fee.
- **Domestic Stock Funds.** Large-cap U.S. stocks have a capitalization (i.e., total value of the corporation) of more than $5 billion. Mid-cap U.S. stocks have a capitalization that ranges from $1 billion to $5 billion. Small-cap U.S. stocks have a capitalization of less than $1 billion.
- **Foreign Stock Funds.** If you want to invest in economies that are growing faster than the U.S. economy, then consider investing in stock funds that include countries like China, India, and Brazil.
- **Bond Funds.** The historical return of stocks can seem so impressive that it makes you wonder why you should bother with bonds. Short-term and intermediate-term bonds mature in less than five

to up to ten years. Long-term bonds mature in ten years or more. Short-term bonds mature in less than five years. Short-term bonds have brief maturities and, therefore, are less volatile than intermediate and long-term bonds because they are more immune to changes in the interest rates.

- **Index Funds.** Index funds are a great alternative to traditional mutual funds not only because they carry lower management fees than actively managed funds, but many consistently outperform them as well. But don't rush out and invest in one until you've checked out what the fund charges for management fees.
- **Individual Stocks.** If your employer is a publically traded company, then there is a good chance one of your 401(k) investment options is company stock.

Review the six investment categories and determine which categories your 401(k) fits into. If you're not sure about a particular option, then place it under the "to-be-determined" category and ask your 401(k) provider to assist you in determining which option applies to your plan.

What Is Your Risk Tolerance Level?

There are different risks associated with each of your investment options. Your tolerance for risk typically goes down as you get older. How do you determine what your risk tolerance is? On your way home from work, do you drive in the slow lane or the fast lane? Each person has a different propensity for risk. When investing, this risk propensity can be used to determine the percentage of your portfolio that is exposed to equities. Find out how you feel about risk by completing the following risk tolerance questionnaire. If you prefer, you can complete an online risk-tolerance questionnaire at calcxml.com, or go to Online Resources at the end of this book to find other risk calculator websites. Check how you've allocated your assets to make sure they line up with the risk level you are comfortable with. If you find a discrepancy, don't be in a rush to immediately change it. Remember, time is on your side, so think about your options before you act.

Risk Tolerance Questionnaire

1. What is your age?

    A. 55 or above
    B. 36–54
    C. 35 years or under

2. What do you expect to be your next major expenditure?

    A. Providing for retirement
    B. Buying a house
    C. Paying for my kids' college education

3. When do you expect to use most of the money you are now accumulating in your investments?

    A. At any time now . . . so a high level of liquidity is important

    B. Probably in the future . . . six to ten years from now

    C. Probably in eleven to twenty years or more from now

4. Over the next several years, you expect your annual income to

    A. stay about the same.

    B. grow moderately.

    C. grow substantially.

5. Due to a general market correction, one of your investments loses 14 percent of its value a short time after you buy it. What do you do?

    A. Sell the investment so you will not have to worry if it continues to decline.

    B. Hold on to it and wait for it to climb back.

    C. Buy more of the same investment, because at the current lower price it looks even better than when you bought it.

6. Which of these investing strategies would you choose for your investment dollars?

    A. You would go for maximum diversity, dividing your portfolio among all available investments, including those ranging from highest return/greatest risk to lowest return/lowest risk.

B. You are concerned about too much diversification, so you would divide your portfolio among two investments with historically high rates of return and moderate risk.

C. You would put your investment dollars in the investment with the highest rate of return and most risk.

7. Assuming you are investing in a stock mutual fund, which one do you choose?

   A. A fund devoted to highly diversified blue-chip stocks that pay dividends

   B. A fund that invests only in established, well-known companies that have a potential for continued growth

   C. A fund of companies that may make significant technological advances that are still selling at their low initial offering price

8. Assuming you are investing in only one bond, which bond do you choose?

   A. A tax-free bond, since minimizing taxes is your primary investment objective

B. The bond of a well-established company that pays a rate of interest somewhere between the other two bonds

C. A high-yield (junk) bond that pays a higher interest rate than the other two bonds, but also gives you the least sense of security with regard to a possible default

9. You expect inflation to return, and it has been suggested that you invest in hard assets such as real estate and cable TV, which have historically outpaced inflation. Your only financial assets are long-term bonds. What do you do?

A. Ignore the advice and hold on to the bonds.

B. Sell the bonds, putting half the proceeds in hard assets and the other half in money market funds.

C. Sell the bonds, put the proceeds in hard assets, and borrow additional money so you can buy even more hard assets.

If you have answered all of the questions, you are ready to determine your estimated risk tolerance level. Start by counting all of your A, B, and C responses. Each A response is worth 1 point, each B response is worth 2 points, and each C response is worth 3 points. Multiply each response by its point value and total your score. For example, if you had two A responses, five B responses, and two C responses, your total score would be 18 (2 + 10 + 6).

TABLE 2.1 ✦ Investment category risk assessment

Category	Risk Level	Objectives
Cash (in interest-bearing accounts)	Conservative	Earn short-term interest rates from secure investments
Domestic Stock Funds	Moderate to aggressive	Speculate on low interest rates to get higher returns at maturity
Foreign Stock Funds	Moderate to aggressive	Follow higher average market returns
Bond Funds	Moderate to aggressive	Invest in stocks, bonds, and commodities with reliable performance over time
Index Funds	Conservative to moderate	Pick a market mix of equities, bonds, and commodities
Individual Stocks	Conservative to aggressive	Select to obtain high rates of returns for shareholders

Possible scores range from a low of 9 to a high of 27. Here are the risk levels that are assigned to the different scores:

Conservative Investor Risk Level (total score: 9 to 14)
Moderate Investor Risk Level (total score: 15 to 20)
Aggressive Investor Risk Level (total score: 21 to 27)

Table 2.1 shows the risk levels generally associated with the six investment categories.

By now you should have an idea of what your investments are, and from Table 2.1 you should know what risk is associated with each. How do your investments match up with your tolerance for risk? If they're right on, great! If there's a discrepancy, do not be too concerned about it. The next section will show you how to use diversity to even out your investments to a comfortable risk level for you.

Diversifying Your Investments

Diversification is the process investors go through to determine what portion of their total investment dollars should be allocated to the investment options available. The goal of diversification is to end up owning a profitable portfolio that will continue to grow in the future to meet your expected returns at a risk you're willing to take.

When you diversify the assets in your portfolio, you lessen the chance of being subjected to the volatility of the market. Your aim is to gather assets that have absolutely nothing in common so that one class of assets will cushion the blow of another class of assets when the market becomes turbulent. In times of financial turbulence, it's highly unlikely that every investment category will behave in the same way. For instance, if stock funds take a nosedive, chances are that bond funds or another category of assets in your portfolio will remain stable.

Diversifying is a way of protecting your portfolio. There are countless investment categories you can use to make that happen. Whether you invest in stock funds, bond funds, or other investments, one of the best ways to reduce the risk of loss in your 401(k) is to spread your money around so that if one investment underperforms, the others may do well and make up for the loss. When you are ready to start diversifying your assets into categories, you can get as simple or as complicated as you like. If you're interested in keeping it simple, then invest in just three mutual funds that invest in domestic stocks, foreign stocks, and bonds.

Choosing Your Options

Deciding what the right investment options are for you is an important part of 401(k) investing. Although it will require some time to set up at the outset, when you're done, you will have learned how it's done, and it will be relatively easy to maintain on a periodic basis. Your first step will be to figure out how big or small each piece of your 401(k) pie will be in different option categories.

The pie charts in Figures 2.1, 2.2, and 2.3 on the following pages illustrate asset diversification for a conservative, a moderate, and an aggressive investor, respectively. Moderates may decide to ease back on stocks to accommodate a greater weight in bonds and fixed income funds. They're willing to sacrifice some potential returns to reduce their exposure to risk. They may also choose to stick to index funds to keep from getting caught up in the market's momentum.

FIGURE 2.1 ◆ Conservative investor

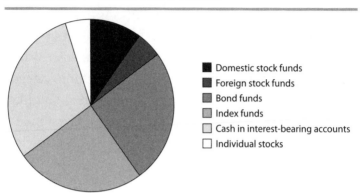

FIGURE 2.2 ◆ Moderate investor

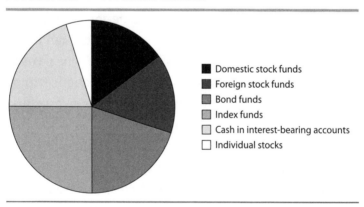

When circumstances that are specific to you occur, you may want to change your allocation. What if your employer has run into financial problems and you fear losing your job? What if your spouse is coping with a medical emergency? If you're dealing with these kinds

FIGURE 2.3 ◆ Aggressive investor

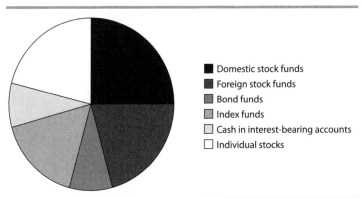

Legend:
- Domestic stock funds
- Foreign stock funds
- Bond funds
- Index funds
- Cash in interest-bearing accounts
- Individual stocks

of situations, it's more important to become conservative and preserve your principal. Or the reverse could happen. What if you just landed the job of your dreams with a huge jump in salary? What if the stock market is doing great? Maybe you can afford to be more aggressive and enjoy a higher rate of return. Those are the kinds of events that will guide you to manage your 401(k) through good and bad times using asset allocation.

Although mid-career workers may be optimistic about making up their 401(k) investment losses incurred from the recession by investing in higher-rate equities, younger workers in their twenties and thirties may take comfort in their respective plans in a depressed stock and mutual fund market with numerous buying opportunities.

Older workers in their fifties and sixties, however, may be in a precarious position. For many, the only option is to work longer to save and allow their investments to recover and decrease the number of years they'll need those savings. Their Social Security benefits will be worth more the longer they wait, up to age 70. In any event, don't assume you will spend less money when you retire. Some people actually spend more, at least during the first few years of retirement as they catch up on home maintenance projects and let loose their pent-up demand to travel.

Every 401(k) plan should include low-cost index funds and target retirement funds. If these options are available to you, your 401(k) will perform far better than most professionally managed funds over the long term. If your plan doesn't include these options, try to get as close to them as you can. Search for funds in your plan that behave most like index funds. The right mix of investment ensures that you're being aggressive enough to earn a decent return without subjecting your money to a level of volatility that is uncomfortable for you. How do you accomplish that? Initially, you may want to accept the percentages the asset allocator calculator dictated.

As we have discussed, asset diversification is crucial to your financial success. And to keep your balance, you have got to be willing to rebalance. For example, let's say you have a 75/25 stock-to-bond allocation. After six months, you discover that stock values are starting to fall dramatically, while bonds are appreciating nicely. It may be time to shift some of your money out of stocks and into bonds. Or the reverse may be happening. The stock market is wildly bullish and bonds are flat. It might be time to take some of your winnings out of stock and store it in a money market fund until the market settles down. Selling your winners is a prudent way to keep your portfolio in good shape. You just have to have the discipline to do it.

When you rebalance, don't be tempted to put everything into the winning asset. As Newton said when he discovered gravity: "Whatever goes up must come down." That scientific axiom is also true of the investment market.

What to Watch Out For

If you discover your 401(k) offers a mishmash of mediocre and expensive funds that don't even cover the basics, consider switching to an IRA. For example, your current plan might offer several large-cap stock funds but not a single small-company or international stock fund. With an IRA, you can fill the gaps in your 401(k) with an almost unlimited number of investment options. Simply do that by opening an IRA and investing some of the money you were tucking away in your 401(k). If your employer isn't matching your 401(k) contributions, then switching to an IRA becomes an easy decision to make. Select investments for your IRA to compensate for the missing links in your 401(k).

Limit your exposure to sales fees as much as possible, and look for mutual funds with low management fees. Management fees are typically charged annually and can exceed 2 percent of the value of your fund. Check the fund's prospectus for commissions and sales charges, as well as management fees before you buy. No-load mutual funds don't charge a sales commission.

Making money in the stock market often involves making the right call about what's about to happen. No one can know the future, but what if you had a way to identify stocks that are on the way up before they attract a lot of attention?

Is it a smart move to invest in your company's stock? Many employees believe that because they work for the company, they are in tune with their company's financial status. Don't let your perceived familiarity overshadow your better judgment. Check the stock out, just as if you were considering investing in XYZ Corporation, a firm you know nothing about. Get a copy of your firm's annual report and read it cover to cover. You'll probably discover some things you didn't know, and if their stock is a good investment, buy some.

Applying What You've Learned

◆ Know exactly what investment options are available in your 401(k) plan and where they fit in the investment categories identified in this chapter.

♦ Determine an investment risk level you're comfortable with and use that to diversify the investments in your 401(k).

♦ Be patient before you make a move to reallocate your investment. Chapters 5, 6, and 7 address in more detail investment strategies for each category.

♦ Remember that age and future financial expenditures are factors in making your decision whether or not to be more conservative or aggressive in your investments.

CHAPTER 3

Know Where You're Going

IF YOU WANT to get to your destination, then you've got to know where you are going. You will have an opportunity in this chapter to put your 401(k) plan through a "retirement readiness test." Your first challenge will be to figure out how much you'll need to retire comfortably. Then you'll need to know how much to save in order to meet that goal. As daunting as that task may seem at the moment, some excellent online tools can help you figure it out. Just make sure that when you use these tools, you enter realistic numbers and assumptions. Otherwise, the numbers you get back will be worthless.

Determining How Much You'll Need

One way to determine what you'll need to live on when you retire is by using one of the many retirement calculators that are on the Internet. A major benefit of using a retirement calculator is that it gives you a reality check on the investment you're making in your 401(k). Will the amount you're saving and investing enable you to accumulate what you'll need for retirement? A good calculator will help you answer this question and find any shortfalls in your retirement plan. Do you need to increase your contributions, adjust your investments to achieve a higher rate of return, or do a combination of both?

Before you start entering data into an online calculator, there are several aspects of your retirement you need to consider. First and foremost is to determine as accurately as you can the monthly retirement income you'll need before you start compiling the rest of your retirement assumptions. Each calculator uses different retirement assumptions, so different calculators can produce different results for you. Check the assumptions each calculator uses to see if they apply to your situation.

Most online calculators will assume an inflation rate of 3 percent to 4 percent, which has been the historical average in the United States over the past several years. Because of the mounting federal budget deficit, many economists expect it will be higher in the future. You can override the calculator's inflation rate with one that you're more comfortable with. The calculator will ask you to enter a flat annual rate of return you expect from your investments.

The inflation percentage that you use to do your calculation assumes that all of your retirement expenses will be impacted by that percentage in retirement. This may not be the case when you retire. For example, some expenses like the cost of gasoline may increase due to inflation. However, if you are no longer commuting to work on a daily basis, the anticipated increase in gas may have a minimal impact on you. Health care costs, however, may have a greater impact on you. If you're covered by Medicare, then perhaps it won't affect you as much as it did when you were working.

You need to determine what your life expectancy will be so the calculator can determine if your 401(k) money will last as long as you will. People are living longer, so you might want to assume a life expectancy to age 95 or 100, which will reduce your chances of outliving your money. These basic assumptions will help you estimate how much money you'll need when you retire and whether you are on track to realize your goal.

Several online calculators are listed in the Online Resources at the end of this book. None of the ones listed require you to register or surrender any personal contact information. They all will produce figures that illustrate how much you'll need to retire, based on the assumptions you've entered. When you start using a calculator, make a quick dry run with rough numbers to get an idea of the information you'll need. Then, gather any information you're missing and repeat the calculation to get more accurate numbers. Here are five excellent calculators to select from that will get you started:

- smartmoney.com/retirement
- mpower.com
- financialengines.com
- morningstar.com
- flexibleretirementplanner.com

Flexibleretirementplanner.com is one of the more sophisticated calculators in that it allows you to distinguish between taxable, tax-deferred, and tax-free assets like Roth IRA accounts. You can also change variables such as income tax rates and spending during retirement. This calculator also determines the probability that, based on your input, you will achieve a comfortable level of retirement factoring the assets you have, your life expectancy, and the economic conditions you'll encounter. You might want to compare the results you get here with those you got using a simpler calculator.

If the results that you get from a calculator are significantly higher than what you expected, don't get discouraged. The problem may be due to an unrealistic assumption. In any event, if the calculator points out a problem you may have with your retirement plan, then take action to resolve it as best you can. The purpose of using the calculator is to help you determine what you can do today to make your retirement years more secure.

Remember that the results from whatever calculator you use are only estimates.

Getting Advice

Preparing a good retirement plan is not easy, but it's essential to your success in retirement. If you have a spouse or partner who'll be joining you in retirement, hold monthly meetings to review where you've been and, more important, where you're going in your plan. List your income and expenses, and openly discuss deviations. What action or steps can you take to get back on track? Identify upcoming expenses as well as your long-term spending goals. Have they, or your priorities, changed?

The rewards that you will realize throughout the remainder of your life will be well worth the time and energy put into your retirement plan. Your financial security is now more on your shoulders than at any time in the past.

Once you've determined how much you will need when you retire, you may want to get some advice on what steps you should take to achieve that financial goal. You need to find a person you feel comfortable with who has the knowledge to provide you with meaningful advice. It may be a knowledgeable friend, or it could be a professional advisor. Advisors often offer complimentary get-acquainted sessions. The National Association of Personal Financial Advisors (NAPFA) offers a questionnaire on their website (napfa.com) that will help you ask the right questions when you interview candidates. Financial Planning Association (fpanet.org) can provide a list of financial planners in your area.

All advisors should focus on your tolerance for risk, your financial goals, and the best way to reach those goals. Make sure you understand their fee structure. To obtain a directory of the financial planners in your area, contact:

- National Association of Personal Financial Advisors, 800-555-6659
- Certified Public Accountants Personal Financial Division, 800-862-4272
- Financial Planning Association, 800-282-7526

When making your initial screening calls, let the potential advisors know as specifically as you can what you need them for and ask what services they offer. Listen carefully to the answers and take notes to help you determine if they have the expertise you need. Ask for the names of at least three clients you can contact for references. Finally, ask how they are paid.

Not everybody can afford or wants to hire a financial advisor. You may be entitled to free or inexpensive advice from the firm that administers your 401(k) and IRA. Companies such as Fidelity Investments, Vanguard, T. Rowe Price, and Charles Schwab offer excellent financial advice and assistance to their clients. Their advisors can often answer common questions regarding your investment and savings goals, asset allocation, and withdrawals from your account. All of these firms maintain outstanding websites that are full of great financial information and tools.

Setting Retirement Goals

When establishing your retirement goals and objectives, you must also establish the level of risk you're willing to accept to meet your investment goals. Ask yourself: "What level of risk am I willing to take with my money to assure that my investment generates high returns?" Your answer to this question is critical because only in fairy tales can you find risk-free investments.

If you're not willing to take risk, don't expect to make impressive returns in your 401(k) plan. You'll have to be content with the returns on your saving account, which will be eaten up by inflation. For example, let's say you invest in thirty-day Treasury bills, which are backed by the full credit of the federal government so you face little chance of losing your money (i.e., they are almost risk free). They will earn about 4 percent annually, which is on par with the rate of inflation. Had you been willing to move across the aisle and invest in a conservative stock fund, you could have realized a return of 8 percent, or twice the Treasury bill's return.

Of course, the reason for the nicer return was because of the greater risk you were willing to take. I'm not advocating loading up your 401(k) portfolio with stock funds, because that would be too risky. A high-risk portfolio isn't necessary to generate worthwhile returns, but you do need to think about how much risk you're comfortable with to meet your retirement goals. As you will see in Chapter 5, there are several ways to control and limit your exposure to risk on high-return investments. There are several free online financial planning tools that are available to anyone, such as TD Ameritrade's Wealth Ruler (tdameritrade.com), Fidelity's My Plan (fidelity.com/myplan), and T. Rowe Price's income calculator (troweprice.com/ric).

Boomer Retirement Strategies

If you were born in any year from 1946 through 1964, then you're considered a baby boomer. The 401(k) losses from the recent recession were more painful to boomers because they have less time to recover as they are just now starting to retire. If you have sustained big losses, you may need to save more, work longer, or do a combination of both.

Even if you're counting the days until you can leave the corporate world and have been burned by the stock market, shunning stocks isn't a good idea. You need to recognize that if you become more conservative, you will have to be willing to save more to meet your retirement goals than someone who's willing to invest more heavily in stocks. There's a price to pay if you're averse to risk. You'll have to give up more of your current income to save for the future.

If you're fortunate to have a pension, you may be able to be more aggressive than someone who has to rely heavily on 401(k) and IRA savings for retirement income. If you don't have a pension, a portfolio of 40 percent stock and 60 percent fixed income may be appropriate. Consider investing 25 percent in blue-chip stocks, 5 percent in small-cap stocks, 10 percent in international stocks, and 60 percent in a combination of bond and money market funds.

Yes, the recession has taken its toll, but fortunately many boomers are in their prime earning years. If you're in this position, try to save as much as possible. Boomers age 50 and older are eligible to make catch-up contributions to their 401(k) and IRA plans. In 2010, workers who are 50 or older can contribute an extra $5,500 to a 401(k).

Generation X Retirement Strategies

You belong to the Generation X group if you were born from 1965 through 1981. In all likelihood, you're just starting to think about retirement, even though it's still years away. So you can afford to recover from the market downturns, even the big scary one we went through starting in 2008. Many workers in their thirties and forties saw their 401(k) plans plummet 25 percent or more during the height of the recession. If you're looking at a thirty- to forty-year time horizon to retire, it's not nearly as bad as you might initially have thought.

For many people, middle age can be an energizing period in their lives. Incomes have hopefully stabilized, and the kids are out of the house or at least getting close to moving on. The ten years preceding retirement offer you an important opportunity to focus on growing your retirement savings by managing your investment now. Check your asset allocation to make sure your accounts are properly organized in taxable and tax-free retirement accounts at dinkytown.com.

A 25 percent drop in your current holdings doesn't mean you'll have 25 percent less for retirement. Depending on how old you are, you can make that up by saving a little more, investing in higher-return equities, or working a little longer. If you're planning on working at least fifteen years or longer, you should probably have about 75 percent of your 401(k) in stock funds. Diversify your 401(k) into 35 percent large-company stock funds, 10 percent into small-company funds, 15 percent in international funds, and 15 percent in bond funds. If you're older, you may want to gradually move toward a mix of 60 percent stock funds and 40 percent bond funds. Remember, you still have time on your side and can afford to take some risk to achieve your retirement goals.

Generation Y Retirement Strategies

If you were born after 1981 you belong to Generation Y. You may not have cared when the market tanked because you didn't have much in it. It afforded you with the opportunity to buy at the bottom, and there was nowhere for the market to go but up. Many of you may have seen your 401(k) holdings rise in value.

Younger workers should invest at least 75 percent of their 401(k)s in stock funds. For moderately aggressive young investors, invest 50 percent in large-company stock funds, 15 percent in small-company funds, 10 percent in foreign funds, and the rest in bond funds. Large-company stocks typically represent where most of the favorable economic activity is in the market. International stock now accounts for 50 percent of the global market. The stock of growing small or mid-size companies can offer a higher return than large-company stocks if your 401(k) plan offers good fund options in these categories.

Retiring Home Free

Assuming you now know how much you'll need to retire, take a deep breath and relax if the amount you'll need was higher than what you expected. Many people assume they'll have to work five or ten years longer than they had planned to build up enough money to retire. But a recent study by Financial Engines (financialengines.com) found that big losses or poor returns on investment don't necessarily translate into declines in projected retirement income. For many, paying off their home mortgages can get them back on course with careful planning.

If you're one of the millions of Americans looking forward to retirement, become a homeowner. If you're already a homeowner, pay off the mortgage as quickly as you can. If you can pay off your home mortgage before you retire, you will have covered 25 percent to 35 percent of your living expenses while you were working and making house payments. That, combined with building up your 401(k) plan, should get you on the road to retirement.

Nothing can save you more money over time than paying off your home mortgage as soon as you can. Typically, homeowners elect to take out thirty-year mortgages because it gives them plenty of time to pay those mortgages off, while offering them lower monthly payments. However, if you're able to increase your monthly mortgage payment by a relatively small amount, you'll pay off your mortgage a lot faster, and it will dramatically improve your retirement picture.

Let's assume that you have a thirty-year $100,000 mortgage at 7 percent, with payments of $665 a month. If you financed the same amount for fifteen years, your monthly payments would be $900, a difference of only $235. You would pay off you home in half the time (fifteen instead of thirty years) and save yourself $80,000 in interest that you can use for retirement. If you can't afford the higher

monthly payment, consider making extra payments whenever you can to accelerate the time it takes to pay it off.

Owning a home is a strategy that deserves special consideration because it can work for you during all the ups
and downs of the economic cycle. During inflationary
periods, home values typically go up at rates that stay even
or beat inflation. Cooling home markets due to the recession and more stringent mortgage qualification standards
have dropped the average prices of homes in many areas.
If you don't own a home, it may be time to consider buying one.

Here's why a home is a smart investment strategy. They
offer one of the best tax shelters (e.g., property tax and
mortgage interest deductions) there is, and if you work it
right, a home that is paid off when you retire can become
the anchor in your retirement plan. Microsoft's website
(realestate.msn.com) covers every step of the home-buying
and owning process from researching neighborhoods to
applying for a mortgage. The site also allows you to visit
more than 500,000 listings throughout the country.

If you're handy with tools and a paint roller, consider
buying a fixer-upper that may be priced 20 percent or 30
percent below the market. Look for distress situations
where the seller has to put a house on the market for a
quick sale because of a foreclosure, job transfer, divorce,
or estate settlement. Never be reluctant to submit an offer
that is substantially less than the asking price. If your
realtor balks, get another one. If you can, buy the cheap-
est house in the neighborhood, because as higher-priced

homes appreciate, they tend to pull up the values of lower-priced homes.

What to Watch Out For

Don't assume you won't live that long when you retire. Go back into a retirement calculator to see the effect adding years to your life has on your finances. Adding even a couple of years will make a big difference. If you project an older age and your retirement finances come up short, consider adding an assumption into your plan for a part-time job or selling your home and downsizing in your later years. Adding home equity into your retirement plan finances may more accurately project what you're worth and make your calculation more realistic.

Retiring early to a less-stressful life can be exciting if you've done all of the calculations and can afford it. However, if you're planning to spend more years in retirement, take extra care to double-check what's available in your retirement accounts. You'll have to wait until you're 59½ to take penalty-free withdrawals from your IRAs.

Pay extra attention to your risk tolerance as you get ready to retire early. The risk tolerance calculator at calcXML (calcxml.com) is a good one to use on an ongoing basis. Measure your risk tolerance at least once a quarter to help you determine how changes in the economy might be affecting you and the way you've allocated your investments. If your portfolio is too volatile, you may be tempted to change your mix of assets, which could reduce the long-term value of retirement accounts. Your age needs to be a bigger factor than your risk tolerance when you retire early.

Applying What You've Learned

◆ Take advantage of online retirement calculators to determine how much you'll need to live comfortably when you retire.

◆ Seek advice and outside help if you feel you need it to assist you in developing your retirement plan.

◆ Establish retirement goals that have specific objectives and target completion dates to help keep you on track for retirement.

◆ Develop a retirement strategy that fits your age.

◆ Buy a home if you don't own one. If you own one, pay off the mortgage as soon as you can to reinforce your retirement plan.

PART 2

INVESTING FOR RETIREMENT

The recent brutal recession is amplifying a longtime concern: Americans don't save nearly enough of their incomes, potentially leaving many to suffer financially in retirement. That's because many feel significant cultural pressure to spend as a way of creating an illusion of affluence. Unfortunately, the process of being spendthrifts is often self-defeating and sabotages retirement plans. Thoughtless spending leaves less money to save and develops lifestyle expectations that can't be maintained in retirement. However, there are glimmers of hope. Recent federal data show in 2009 the U.S. personal savings rate has climbed to 5 percent of disposable income, up from less than 2 percent. Most financial experts say American workers should ideally save at least 10 percent or more of their gross incomes to achieve a secure retirement.

CHAPTER 4

Finding the Money You'll Need

WHETHER THE RECESSION has hit you directly or not, now is the time to look at ways to save everything you can for your retirement. There are literally hundreds of books with thousands of ways to save money. In this chapter, all of that "how to save" clutter has been consolidated into a few concise pages to help you find the additional money you may need to supplement your retirement plan.

Where to Look

One of the best ways to ensure that you will come away from this chapter with money in your pocket is to arrange to have any savings that you identify automatically transferred from your checking to a savings account each month. Transferring the money keeps you from spending it on something you don't need, and you'll be richer for doing it. Here are other ideas for finding money:

♦ **Lower your insurance premiums.** Shop around for less expensive auto, home, and life insurance. If you have low deductibles, find out how much you would save by increasing them. Increasing the deductible on car collision insurance from $250 to $500 can save 20 percent or more. Make sure you aren't overinsured.

♦ **Reduce your telephone and cable expenses.** Switching from an unlimited calling plan to one with a fixed number of minutes per month is one way to reduce your telephone bill. Eliminate the premium TV channels you never watch.

♦ **Cut your grocery bill.** Shop once as opposed to several times during the week because the more trips you make to the store, the more likely you are to make impulse purchases. Stop drinking bottled water, and buy a filter for your faucet. Buy only food that's in season. Out-of-season produce can cost 25 percent to 50 percent more.

♦ **Cut your gasoline bill.** Drive to work with a colleague or find someone online at carpoolworld.com or erideshare.com. Burn regular gas instead of premium if your car will accept it, but check your owner's manual first. Combine trips or ride your bike.

◆ **Cut your cleaning costs.** Most clothes that are dry-cleaned can be washed by hand or in a washing machine.

◆ **Trim your kids' college expenses.** College books cost a fortune if bought new. Rent them for a fraction of the cost from campusbookrentals.com or chegg.com.

◆ **Negotiate lower credit card rates.** Call your credit card's customer service and tell them you're planning to transfer your balance unless you get a lower rate. Compare rates at cardratings.com or billshrink.com.

◆ **Reduce your energy bills.** If your utility company offers it, get a free energy audit on your home or do it yourself using the guide at energystar.gov. Set a programmable thermostat that you can buy for less than $50 to automatically lower the heat or raise the temperature of the air conditioner after bedtime and when you're not home. Use florescent bulbs, which require 75 percent less energy and last ten times longer than incandescent ones.

◆ **Shop online.** If you want to buy a high-end item without having to pay a high-end price, shop online at bluefly .com, yoox.com, or ebay.com. There are numerous other reputable sites available. Many local retailers will match Internet prices rather than lose business.

◆ **Have fun for a lot less.** Go to a minor-league ball game, and you'll probably pay 20 percent of what it would have cost you for major-league tickets. Cut back on eating out and eliminate fast-food places.

◆ **Watch how you use credit cards.** Pay with cash or use a debit card for everyday purchases like groceries. Create a payoff plan for each of your credit cards. When you pay off a card, cut it in half and cancel it. When you start paying with cash, you'll find yourself passing up impulse purchases.

◆ **Automatically deposit any extra money you get.** When you get a raise, deposit the extra money directly into a savings account so you'll never miss it. Do the same thing with part-time money, bonuses, or overtime pay. When you get an income-tax refund, use it to pay off a credit card. Then cancel the card and deposit the money you were paying on the card into your savings account.

Little expenses can add up quickly, so be creative at finding the money you're wasting. Make gradual changes that are easier to stick with. Start taking lunches to work instead of eating out; you'll be amazed at how much you'll save. You'll also feel a lot better. Have raises and bonuses automatically deposited into a savings account. If you finally paid off your car loan and there's still several years left in the old clunker, invest what you were paying for the installment loan.

Spend Less

To spend less, you first must know what you're spending now. Although this may sound like a no-brainer, many people don't fully comprehend that they spend more money than they make. Having done the retirement calculations in Chapter 3, you should have a good idea of how much you'll need to accumulate before retirement. You also have to have a clear idea of what you actually need versus the luxury items that you simply want. Your answers to the following three questions will help clarify the difference between needs and wants:

1. If I buy it, will I still be using it in five years?

2. Is it something that I'm buying just to keep up with the lifestyle of my friends?

3. Will this purchase help me reach my retirement goal?

Holding regular financial management meetings with your partner or a friend is one way to help get over the excessive spending hurdle. Ask the same three questions

in those meetings, and take note of your and your partner's answers. Any decision you make to allocate more
money to retirement savings will probably require lifestyle changes.

Create a Savings Goal

Set a goal to save at least 10 percent of your income in a
401(k) plan and other tax-sheltered retirement accounts.
If you can't save 10 percent, start by saving 1 percent. Once
you get used to the idea of consistently saving 1 percent,
take the next step and make it 2 percent. There is no need
to stop when you get to 10 percent. If you're able to save
even more, you will be that much better off at retirement.
Take whatever action you need to take to avoid living on
your entire paycheck. An aggressive savings plan will help
you do that.

It may seem like the amount you're able to put toward
your 401(k) plan is too small to make a difference, but
every little bit counts. Small amounts consistently saved
will accumulate fast. Starting to save early captures the
amazing power of compound interest. To see how it works,
let's assume that you deposited $1,000 a year into your
401(k) and that it earned 5 percent interest over eleven
years. During that time, your total deposits of $11,000
would be worth a whopping $23,000. That's because each
year's interest on your savings is added to your principal,
thereby generating still more interest of its own.

Saving money on a regular basis will play a huge role in getting you ready for retirement. If you find yourself living from paycheck to paycheck, then the prospect of saving anything may seem remote. Unfortunately, if you can't figure out a way to save something for retirement, then your plan to retire won't happen on your terms.

Get Rid of Debt

Should you save money or pay off your debts first? A lot of people aren't in the enviable position of having the financial ability to do both. The die-hard savers will argue that the more money they have in savings, the better they can survive a financial emergency without running up more debt. The opposing debt-killers will argue that the amount of interest they'll earn in a savings account is insignificant in comparison to the interest they're paying on loans. Who's right? Both are. However, everyone needs to develop the discipline it takes to save, even if it's a small amount while paying off debts.

Some financial advisors will encourage you to pay off smaller debts first regardless of their interest rates to reduce your number of debts faster. Others say you should consider consolidating all of your credit card debts into one that offers you a balance transfer option. However, the consolidation option opens up the temptation of adding more debt to the very cards that got you in trouble in the first place.

It makes financial sense to pay off your higher interest rate debts first because those are the ones that are costing you the most. To get started, organize your outstanding loans from the highest to the lowest interest rate. If you are able to do it, increase the amount of your payments against your high interest rate loans first to get them paid off. Then once a loan is paid off, use that money to increase the payment you're making on the next highest interest rate loan.

When you pay off a high-interest credit card, destroy it. After you've cut it up into small pieces, three wonderful things will happen. First, you'll start buying less of what you really don't need. According to a recent study, credit cards account for more than 50 percent of the impulse-buying patterns of shoppers. Second, your total debt will start to shrink exponentially. As high-interest cards get paid off, you will end up with money you didn't know you had for investing into your 401(k) or IRA accounts. Finally, once you're out of debt, you will feel great. Keep just one or two cards to cover yourself for financial emergencies only. When you can consistently pay the balance off at the end of each month, you will know you've kicked the credit card habit for good.

There are a number of online repayment plan calculators at websites like quicken.com. Quicken's Debt Reduction Planner is an excellent get-out-of-debt planning tool. Similar tools are available in personal finance software applications that are available at local computer supply stores for $25 to $50.

Set Up a Budget

Everyone should have a budget, even millionaires. It's crucial to know where your money is coming from and where it is going. By monitoring your spending habits, you will begin to identify areas where cost savings can occur. Your budget then becomes a valuable tool you can use to help you get out of debt, keep your spending on track, and find the extra money for your 401(k) plan. Many consider budgeting to be a tedious task, but it really doesn't have to be. Once you set up your budget, it can be easy and even fun to maintain. There are several primary components to a good monthly budget.

♦ Disposable income is your gross income less withholding taxes, health insurance, and 401(k) contribution. If you decide to work part-time, add that income to the mix as well. Your retirement income will probably include Social Security, any pension income, income from your investments, and withdrawals from savings and retirement plans.

♦ Major expenses are usually contractual, such as rent or mortgage payments, car loans, property taxes, and day care. These are the expenses that you must pay before you consider other expenses.

♦ Credit card payments are the total monthly payments you need to make on all your cards.

◆ Necessities are important expenses such as groceries, utilities, and home maintenance that can be adjusted through tight money management techniques.

◆ Discretionary expenses can be significantly modified or eliminated altogether and include entertainment, take-out food, pocket money, and so on.

◆ Savings is the final component of the budget and shows what you'll do with any money that's left over after all expenses have been paid.

Write a list of all your expenses over the past several months. Use your checking account records and credit card records to make sure you include everything. Then, divide the list into three categories: must pay expenses, like to have expenses, and don't really need expenses. Carefully evaluate every expense on the "don't need" part of your list.

Although these steps may seem pretty simple, taking action is what separates the "gonna-doers" from the "doers" every time. Pay yourself first. As soon as you get your paycheck, make it a habit of immediately writing a check out to your savings account and depositing it. Better yet, if your employer offers an automatic payment deposit feature into your savings account, take it.

If you want to maintain your budget on your personal computer, there are several online sites you can use, such as simpleplanning.net. Some banks also offer this service at no charge if you have a checking account with them. If you don't have an expense-tracking system or don't like the one you're using, try the one at yodlee.com or mint .com to get started. There are several free online budgeting sites, such as wesabe.com, that can help you get through the budgeting process. Lendingtree.com offers an Advice & Calculators option that will help you track what you're spending.

Whatever system you use should give you a quick picture of your overall expenses and make it easier to gain control over out-of-control expenses. This step is essential to make room in your budget for investing in your retirement. When you complete this process, you may be surprised to see exactly where your money is going each month. You'll discover places where you can cut back to come up with the money you need to save.

Once you are comfortable with your monthly budget, go through your list of expenses and check off those expenses that will likely go down when you retire, such as commuting expenses, lunches at work, and so on. Next, mark those expenses that will likely go up when you retire, like health care.

Earn Extra Money

Yes, you are working hard to meet your retirement goal, but sometimes the only way you can get there is to earn some extra money. According to the Bureau of Labor Statistics, four of ten Americans are working a second job. Moonlighting—holding a second job in addition to a regular one—can take on many different forms. Looking for a part-time job is much like the steps you went through to find your full-time job. Scan the classified job ads and surf Internet job boards for leads. Be sure to check out the temporary services as well. When the regular job market is weak, the temporary job market can compensate for the difference. Temporary jobs cut across all occupations and time slots.

If you're thinking about starting a home-based business, you can order *The Small Business Catalog* for free by calling 800-947-7724. Home business guides, which cost about $40 each, are featured in the catalog. You can also order videos of the home businesses featured. Each guide shows you how to start up a specific home business. It's an inexpensive way to review what the editors consider are the best home business opportunities.

Businesses You Can Start, a great book published by Adams Media, features five hundred start-up businesses complete with cost and earnings estimates. It will even help you create a dynamic business plan for your home business. You need to identify your target market with a clear definition of who will most likely be your customers—the ones who will buy your products or services. Decide how you will reach them (e.g., ads) and how you will sell to them. Your plan should include a three-year cash flow projection showing monthly estimates for income, expenses, and profits.

Always have a separate telephone number and e-mail address for your home business. You won't impress potential or existing customers who call and get an answer from a family member not associated with your business. Use a separate e-mail address that identifies the name of your business rather than your own name. Your business must be able to accept payment from Visa and MasterCard. Yes, there is a service fee for using these cards, but you don't want to turn down a sale because you can't accept a customer's card.

If you have a limited background in accounting, then get a good accountant to help you out, even if you have to pay for it. An accountant can show you how to keep track of your income and expenses and potentially save you thousands of dollars by taking legitimate tax deductions. Keep your accounting records straight by keeping receipts for all business expenses.

Applying What You've Learned

- Use your imagination to look everywhere to cut expenses and save toward retirement.
- Make it a habit to start spending less. Don't buy things you really don't need.
- Set a goal to consistently start saving something, even if it's a small amount. It's critical that you establish the discipline to save now for later.

- ◆ Make a concerted effort to eliminate debt as much as possible, and invest the dollars you'll save into your 401(k) account.
- ◆ Every time you get paid, write a check out to yourself first and deposit it into your savings account before you pay any of your bills.
- ◆ Use everything you've learned in this chapter to set up a monthly budget that you religiously maintain.

CHAPTER 5

Making Good Investments

NO ONE LIKES to lose money, especially if it is more than you can afford. The amount of investment risk you're willing to take may depend on how soon you'll need the money—your time horizon to retire. If you have twenty or more years to go, then it may not bother you if the stock market goes into a slump for a couple of years, because you have the time to wait it out. But if you need the money in five years or less, you may not have the time to wait for the market to recover. This is the time when you need to move from high-risk to low-risk investments such as certificates of deposit (CDs) to protect your retirement dollars. Don't let yourself get caught in the trap of thinking that you're diversifying when you buy a stock fund instead of an individual stock. That won't help if the entire market takes a nosedive. Although younger investors may have the time to pick themselves up and start over, doing so becomes more difficult as you get older.

Even if you've assembled a portfolio of good solid performers, we're still at the mercy of an economic downturn, as was vividly illustrated in the recession that hit in 2008. Before you rush to pull all your 401(k) money out of stock funds, understand that there is no such thing as a completely risk-free investment.

Even savings accounts protected by the Federal Deposit Insurance Corporation (FDIC) are only insured up to a certain amount. Cash in your retirement accounts should have either FDIC or Securities Investor Protection Corporation (SIPC) insurance coverage. The FDIC insurance protects up to $250,000 of your cash if the bank holding your deposit fails. Coverage is limited to $250,000 per person at each individual bank. If you have a $250,000 CD at Bank A and $250,000 deposited in a money market fund at Bank B, each account would be fully insured.

There are two types of instruments to invest in: debt and equity investments. Debt investments are essentially where you loan money to an entity for a specific period of time. In return, you earn interest on the loan and get your principal back at the end of the loan term or the loan maturity date. Examples of debt instruments are CDs, money market funds, and bonds. Equity refers to the stock market. When you make an investment in equity, you're buying a piece of a company (stock), or if it's a stock mutual fund, you're investing in a share of several companies held by the fund. The amount you gain or lose depends on how well the company or companies do in the stock market.

Timing the Market

We have all heard stories about people losing their entire retirement savings. In some cases, it happened overnight, but many just lost their savings over time. After watching much of their 401(k) savings evaporate over the past several years with traditional buy-and-hold strategies, many people are determined not to leave what's left over to the mercy of the investment gods.

Although you'll probably never lose all your money even if it's all invested in the stock market, you will significantly increase your exposure to risk if you don't periodically monitor the well-being of your investments. Losses will occur if you fail to take corrective action when the times warrant it, a process called timing the market. Timing the market means determining at a particular moment in time which way the market is going—up or down.

Trying to time the market is something the "experts" say you can't do. Instead, the implication is that you're supposed to invest blindly in the market, hoping that everything will work out over time. However, if you don't have a sense of market timing before and after you make an investment decision, hang on for the ride!

In spite of what the experts say you can't do, you can time the market. To show you how to do that, play a version of the Monday morning quarterback game with me. That's a game where all the football fans gather around the watercooler on Monday mornings and tell anyone who is willing to listen what their team should have done to win the game on Sunday. It's the old hindsight to foresight game that many of us have either participated in or listened to as others played it.

Let's play Monday morning quarterback with your 401(k) plan. Flash back to March 2008 for a moment and assume that you're about to invest $10,000 of your 401(k) money into one of the ten largest and most prestigious stock funds that existed at that time. Pick your favorite one from this "top ten" list:

- American Capital World Growth (CWGIX)
- American Euro Pacific Growth (AEPGX)
- American Growth Fund of America (AGTHX)
- Davis New York Venture (NYTVX)
- Dodge & Cox Stock (DODGX)
- Fidelity Contrafund (FCNTX)
- Fidelity Diversified International (FDIVX)
- Franklin Income (FKINX)
- Vanguard 500 Index (VFINX)
- Vanguard Total Stock Market Index (VTSMX)

Let's assume you invested $10,000 into the fund you picked because you were sure that it would be a winner.

Now fast-forward to March 2009, and check Table 5.1 to see how your fund performed from March 2008 through March 2009.

On average, your $10,000 stake in any one of the ten funds would be worth only about $7,000. Your fund lost, on average, 30 percent of your investment, and you are not a happy fan standing by the watercooler on Monday morning listening to your friends tell you how they too lost betting on the funds they chose. Could you have prevented that from happening? Yes, if you had access to some basic market timing information at the time.

TABLE 5.1 ◆ Ten stock fund performances

Fund Name	3/2008–3/2009 Return
American Capital World Growth (CWGIX)	−31.5%
American Euro Pacific Growth (AEPGX)	−29.9%
American Growth Fund of America (AGTHX)	−30.4%
Davis New York Venture (NYTVX)	−33.2%
Dodge & Cox Stock (DODGX)	−36.5%
Fidelity Contrafund (FCNTX)	−30.3%
Fidelity Diversified International (FDIVX)	−38.0%
Franklin Income (FKINX)	−22.7%
Vanguard 500 Index (VFINX)	−31.2%
Vanguard Total Stock Market Index (VTSMX)	−31.1%
Average Return	−30.0%

Suppose you had access to a simple graph that shows what direction the stock market is going at any moment in time. (See Figure 5.1.) If you review the information that's displayed on the graph, you can readily determine which way the market was heading as it approached the summer of 2008. Was that the time to sell the stock fund

FIGURE 5.1 ♦ Dow Jones Industrial Average (DIA) January 2008–March 2009

you bought in March 2008? Even if you had bought any one of the "top ten" funds on the list, it should have been painfully clear that you should get out of the stock market and incur only a small loss, rather than incurring a major loss (i.e., 30 percent) by waiting until March 2009.

There's an old saying among Wall Street veterans: "Never try to catch a knife or the market when it's coming down or you'll cut yourself." The point of the Monday morning quarterback game was to show that with access to basic market timing information, you stand a better chance of making rational investment decisions than you would if you're playing the game blindfolded.

Fortunately, you do have access to several online tools that can point you to a wealth of market timing information like that in Figure 5.1. I used an index fund that's traded on the New York Stock Exchange under the trade symbol DIA (Dow Industrial Average) for that figure. (Index funds are covered in Chapter 7.)

The ten mutual funds that I used in my timing-the-market illustration were all invested in large-cap stocks trading on the New York Stock Exchange as well. It makes sense that if I had invested in one of those funds, I would want to follow the market trend, the Dow Jones Industrial Average (DIA) affecting the value on any one of the ten funds I may have selected in the game.

The downtrend graphically illustrated by DIA would have warned me about the sudden downturn that was occurring in the market (i.e., market timing), and I could have sold the fund and substantially reduced my losses

instead of waiting until March 2009. I used stockcharts
.com to create the DIA graph. Since DIA is traded on
the New York Stock Exchange as an exchange traded
fund, anybody has access to its performance record. It's
an online site that allows you to create free charts of any
stock, index fund, or mutual fund in their database. (See
Figure 5.2.)

   Successful market timing requires three key ingre-
dients: a reliable signal to tell when to get in and out of

FIGURE 5.2 ◆ DIA exchange traded fund market performance

stocks, mutual funds, and bonds; the ability to interpret the signal correctly; and the discipline to act on it. The popular image of market timing is that it calls for making drastic, all-or-nothing moves into and out of a particular market. In reality, market timers adjust their investments in stages that don't reflect a black-and-white view of the market.

While some market timers may trade frequently, others change from buy to sell or vice versa on occasion. In any case, pulling out of the market during its most uncertain period results in a smoother and more profitable ride for your 401(k) portfolio compared to a buy-and-hold approach. Table 5.2 includes a number of other index funds that, like DIA, track different segments of the market that you may be invested in or are thinking about investing in; use them to help time the market.

Using Online Tools

Hundreds of websites feature nearly every tool imaginable for investors to use. Since there clearly isn't enough room here to cover them all, I have narrowed the selection to several excellent sites that you may want to visit. Additional sites are listed in Online Resources.

Stockcharts.com allows you to use their stock and mutual fund charting tools at no charge. For a fee, you can access the site's more sophisticated charting capabilities and features. For example, their performance charts

TABLE 5.2 ◆ Market-tracking index funds

Trade Symbol—Fund Name	What the Fund Tracks
DSG—DOW JONES SMALLCAP GROWTH	It seeks to replicate the returns of the Dow Jones Wilshire Small Cap Growth Index.
DSV—DOW JONES SMALLCAP VL	The fund primarily invests in companies that replicate the performance of the Dow Jones Wilshire Small Cap Value Index.
IRY—S&P HEALTH CARE	The fund seeks to replicate the Standard & Poor's 500 Stock Index.
XLK—TECHNOLOGY	It is composed of companies involved in such industries as Internet software, information technology, and computers.
XLI—INDUSTRIAL	This fund mainly invests in an array of industrial companies, including aerospace, defense, and building.
XLE—ENERGY SELECT	It mainly invests in companies that primarily develop and produce crude oil and natural gas.
XLF—FINANCIAL SELECT	The fund invests in an array of financial service firms with diversified business lines ranging from commercial to investment banking.

XLU—UTILITIES SELECT	This fund invests in companies that produce, generate, transmit, or distribute electricity or natural gas.
XLV—HEALTHCARE	It invests in the companies that replicate the performance of companies listed on Standard & Poor's Health Care Select Sector Index.
KBE—KBW BANK	It invests in stocks of companies operating in the banking sector and regional banking institutions.
FEZ—DJ EURO STOCKS	The fund invests in European equity markets, including Finland, France, Germany, Italy, Netherlands, and Spain.
SPY—S&P DEP RECEIPTS	It invests in the growth stocks of large-cap companies. The fund seeks to replicate the performance of the Standard & Poor's 500 Stock Index.

let you compare the performances of sets of securities over various periods of time. You can also scan a collection of stocks or funds to spot buying or selling (i.e., market timing) signals in the market.

Fidelity.com is available to you even if you're not a Fidelity Investment client. The right side of their home page shows you graphically how today's market is doing and what stocks are the top market movers. You can get a detailed stock quote by entering the trade name in the quote box. Their tools and calculator options are located in the center of the home page. Fidelity specializes in mutual funds, so its site features numerous articles and information about specific funds.

Vectorvest.com is the corporate site of VectorVest Inc., which specializes in providing their members with a variety of excellent market timing tools along with a stock rating system that is nothing short of outstanding. They charge a monthly fee for access to their site with an introductory offer of $9.95. If you're interested in learning more, call 888-658-7638.

Smartmoney.com offers free investment reports and a full set of investment tools. Their site also allows you to set up a watch list of stocks that can be tracked daily, if you want.

Money.com is a first-class website that offers numerous features and a wide array of timely articles and information covering all aspects of living, including retiring worry free and finding the best places to live.

Schwab.com offers a limited number of features to nonclient inquiries. A discount brokerage firm that has maintained an excellent reputation, Charles Schwab offers comments about the latest market trends at its website.

As their site name implies, Timingthemarket.net specializes in providing site visitors with the latest information and their editorial opinions of where the market is going. The site also includes an education section, comments on notable stocks, and a technical talk forum.

Separating Winners from Losers

Successfully investing in the market means more than being in it at the right time. It means being in the right places as well. A key to your success will be to determine which industry sectors are in the best position to cash in on the economic recovery. For example, if stocks are following a pattern of recovery, look at the ones that were most exposed to the economy's ups and downs, such as financial services, technology companies, and consumer discretionary companies that make big-ticket items like appliances.

To figure out which sectors will be future winners, study the past. Over the past fifty years, certain sectors have enjoyed their best times during particular points in an economic recovery. Look for solid performance in funds that invest in discretionary stocks but also are in manufacturers. Companies that manufacture products will start using up their inventories as demand picks up. When that happens, they need to order materials to create more goods to sell. The sectors to watch out for are those that are dependent on consumers going back to their old free-spending habits. You may want to hold fewer U.S. stock funds and more foreign stock funds as a way to profit from faster growth abroad in places like China.

Bond fund prices fall when interest rates rise. And a big supply of Treasury bonds with fewer buyers could push interest rates higher. The Chinese, who are one of the largest buyers of Treasury securities, are buying fewer Treasuries.

Conservative investors should look for high-quality bond funds that hold bonds that mature in two to five years. Any money you keep in money market funds will not earn as much as bond funds. You can also earn a decent rate of return by moving into a short-term certificate of deposit (CD). Our huge federal deficit boosts the odds of a surge in the inflation rate in the coming years. Consider Treasury bonds, which go up in price when inflation rises. Utility stock funds and commodity funds are also good inflation hedges.

If you're willing to look beyond the market-beating that a lot of funds were victim to over the past couple of years, there are still some plausible reasons to build an active portfolio. To minimize market volatility, buy only cash-rich stock funds that hold blue-chip stocks. For larger gains, invest in a fund that holds fast-growing small companies. In other words, use active funds to fine-tune your portfolio so that it fits with your risk tolerance.

Assessing the Risk-Reward Relationship

There is a reward you will realize if you're willing to take on more risk. You need to choose reasonable investments that fit into your financial goals for retirement and satisfy your tolerance for risk. Two investments with different levels of risk can produce very different rewards. For example, Figure 5.3 illustrates how much of a favorable impact an additional 3 percent return will have on your 401(k) plan.

FIGURE 5.3 ♦ Comparison of 6 versus 9 percent investment over thirty years

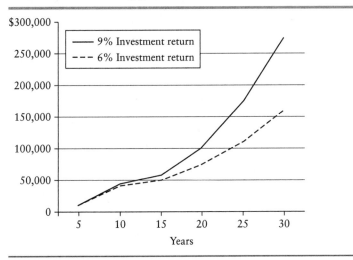

Figure 5.3 compares two hypothetical investments with different risk levels. The one with the higher risk has a 3 percent higher annual return than the one with a lower risk—9 percent versus 6 percent. But, look at the large difference in the end balance of $275,000 for the 9 percent return versus $160,000 for the 6 percent return over thirty years. The 3 percent higher return generates a 75 percent higher return, or $115,000 more.

When it comes to investing, the amount of risk you can tolerate has nothing to do with whether you like skydiving or driving fast cars. It has more to do with your time horizon to retirement and the amount of time you're willing to expend monitoring your investments. Can you handle a 10 percent, 25 percent, or even bigger drop in the value of your 401(k)? Your answer will help you determine whether to invest in risky stock funds or safer bond funds. Imagine the $100,000 in your 401(k) drops to $50,000 in value. Would you be able to hang on, or, in anguish, would you put the money you have left in lower-risk investments? If you sell your high-risk bond fund, you'll have to dramatically increase your contribution to make up for both the loss and the lower investment return you will get from the bond fund.

Many investors are comfortable owning high-risk stock funds when the market is doing well but tend to sell when the market takes a nosedive. But they know how to manage their risk level. Let's repeat the scenario where you had invested $100,000 in a high-risk stock fund. You had determined you were comfortable with a 10 percent risk level and were willing to actively monitor the investment in your portfolio. When the stock market starts to take a nosedive, you do what every 401(k) participant has a right to do: you sell your stock fund and buy a lower-risk investment, thereby limiting your loss to just $1,000 (based on the $100,000 investment example).

The whole point of finding a comfortable risk level is that it helps you stick to your retirement plan. By investing in and managing high-risk investments, you have the opportunity to enjoy higher returns if you are willing to take the time to monitor the market's upsides and downsides. If you're not willing to do this, then choose a good, solid low-risk investment that typically generates a lower return. But remember that if you invest too conservatively, your money may not grow enough to offset inflation. Even though you're earning some return, prices may be rising faster because of inflation, leaving you with less spending power when you retire. On the other hand, if you invest too aggressively, the ups and downs may be more than you can stand.

Tracking Your Investments

Knowing how your 401(k) investments are doing at any moment in time is critical to the overall management of your plan. Tracking your portfolio investments lets you see if they will eventually reach the results you're looking for, in your time frame. This is important for two reasons. You can better predict what the future performance of the portfolio may be by knowing how it has been performing. Tracking also ensures you own a variety of investment categories to reduce risk while maintaining or increasing your expected returns.

Fortunately, there are a number of online portfolio investment tracking tools available, as listed in Online Resources. Figure 5.4 illustrates how a portfolio tracking tool can be used to show how your investments are doing.

Using Brokers

In 2007, the Harvard School of Business conducted a study examining the performance of thousands of broker-sold mutual funds and comparing them to funds that were purchased by individual investors. One would assume that the funds sold by the brokers outperformed the funds that were selected by individuals. A quick review of the study's findings tells a different story. The individual investors earned an annual return of nearly 11 percent as compared to 8 percent for the brokers' clients.

Why did the brokers lag so badly? That's because some brokers are more interested in their own wallets than their clients' wallets. They may select funds that their bro-

FIGURE 5.4 ◆ Example of an online portfolio

Portfolio Summary for VVTop10 as of - 7/30/2009

Buy From Search	Investment	$100,000.00
Short From Search	Equity	$36,210.00
Sell When...	Buying Power	$169,171.90
Cover When...	Interest	$0.00
< Update >	Net	$2,690.95
9 /30/2009 ▾	Cash	$66,480.95
ViewType	Total Value	$102,690.95
Portfolio View ▾	Margin	$0.00
	Gain/Loss %	2.69%

Company	Symbol	Purchase Date	Type	Cost / Share	Last	Gain / Share	REC	Quantity	Cost Basis	Market Value	Gain
ClickSoftware	CKSW	7/17/2009	Long	$7.76	$7.78	$0.02	B	1000	$7,759.95	$7,780.00	$20.05
Kirkland's Inc	KIRK	7/17/2009	Long	$13.76	$13.54	-$0.22	B	1000	$13,759.95	$13,540.00	-$219.95
Medifast Inc	MED	7/17/2009	Long	$14.36	$14.89	$0.53	B	1000	$14,359.95	$14,890.00	$530.05

kerage firm is pushing them to sell and that pay them the highest fee. They can also be guilty of chasing what's hot today, rather than recommending funds that are a good fit in your short- or long-term retirement plan.

So why are investors willing to pay large brokers' fees for questionable returns? Individual investors often assume that brokers know more about what they're doing than they do. In most of their dealings with their clients, brokers aren't considered fiduciaries. A fiduciary is ethically bound to put the client's interest first as opposed to personal interest.

If you are working with a broker, make sure he or she is living up to your expectations. If your broker puts you into trendy investments that tank, find another broker. Good ones will help you build long-term investment plans in concert with your risk tolerance. Be wary of the broker who always wants you to invest in a fund that his or her firm has picked. If the broker has a "preferred" list, make sure he or she can explain to your satisfaction why each investment is preferred and what the risks are.

What does it take to enter your own trade online instead of using a broker? The simple answer is about one minute of your time. You basically enter the fund's trade abbreviation, like FTCNX; enter the dollar amount you want to invest in the fund; and press the enter key. (See Figure 5.5.)

The fees that you pay when you buy individual stocks or funds online are typically 10 percent or less of what

FIGURE 5.5 ✦ Example of an online stock order screen

Symbol	IBM Find Symbol Get Quote
Action	Buy ▼
Quantity	100 Shares
Order Type	Market Order ▼
Time in Force	Day ▼
Conditions	None ▼

you'd pay a broker. Of course, when you order online, you presumably have done all of the appropriate research on your investment choice before entering the order.

What to Watch Out For

There's the story about a great know-it-all who liked to say, "The only time I ever made a mistake was when I *thought* I had made a mistake." Few would argue with the assertion that learning from our mistakes is a central component of self-improvement. To become a savvy investor, you need to put a high premium on knowing the investment mistake that you don't want to make.

Beware of over-concentrating your investments. You need to be willing to not over-invest in your favorite fund and instead diversify the investments in your portfolio. Don't forget to look at the big picture. We sometimes ignore the economic forecasts and focus exclusively on selecting investments that were susceptible to a downturn in the economy. Expect the unexpected, and don't assume that everything will resolve itself over time.

Book your profits. It's easy to be mesmerized when your investments are appreciating. Each uptick provides you with a further conviction of your wisdom and success. However, whatever you bought that's going up will probably come down. Taking profits is rarely a cause for regret. Stay humble. If the 2008 recession taught you nothing else, it should have taught you that disciplined self-doubt is a vital part of the investment process.

Applying What You've Learned

- Timing the market means determining at a particular moment in time which way the market is going—up, down, or sideways.
- Hundreds of websites feature investment tools you can use. Several excellent sites are listed in Online Resources at the end of this book.
- You need to be cognizant of the market's ups and downs. Don't be afraid to take risks, but be prepared to pull out of an investment that may cost you more money in the long run.

◆ The more risk you're willing to take, the more return you'll realize. Choose reasonable investments that fit into your financial goals for retirement and satisfy your tolerance for risk.

◆ If you are working with a broker, make sure he or she is living up to your expectations. Just remember, the fees for buying individual stocks or funds online are typically 10 percent or less than paying a broker to do it.

CHAPTER 6

Investing in Stock Funds and Bond Funds

PEOPLE OFTEN ASK me what return to expect from their 401(k)s. That's a tough question, and I wish I could answer it definitively, but I can't. Why? Because the return on your 401(k) investments depends on a number of factors, including the risk level you're comfortable with. Investing more aggressively (taking more risk) in stocks, for example, gives a greater chance of higher returns. Conversely, investing in bonds is thought to be less risky and subsequently offers lower returns. This chapter covers investing in stock funds and bond funds as well as where to find quality funds to help reduce your risk exposure.

Stock Fund Basics

Stock funds are made up of a diversified pool of stocks that are professionally managed. They're popular with people who are not interested in picking individual stocks for portfolios. The fund's managers do that for you either on an active or passive management basis. Actively managed funds employ managers who are constantly evaluating the market and selecting investments they believe will outperform others.

Passively managed funds follow the logic that it's unlikely active fund managers will beat the market over the long term. Therefore, passively managed funds seek simply to match the performance of the market over the short and long term by buying investments that replicate a particular market's index. You pay a higher fee for actively managed stock funds than you do for passively managed funds.

Domestic stock funds can be made up of a mix of large-cap, mid-cap, and small-cap U.S. stocks, or they can be made up exclusively from one of those three categories. Foreign stock funds typically invest in economies that are growing faster than ours, like those of China, India, and Brazil.

The volatile environment hasn't been kind to stock funds. The average diversified equity fund had returned 12 percent before the market started to crash in the summer of 2008. Since then, that tally has been cut by more than half to 4.25 percent as every major fund category has taken it on the chin. Small-company stock funds have been particularly hard-hit.

Why Invest in Stock Funds?

Over the past ten years, investors who bet on stock funds lost more than 20 percent of their holdings, while those who wagered on bond funds saw their money nearly double. So why buy stocks funds? If you believe the stock market will fully restore itself, equities will offer higher returns for assuming greater risk than if you buy bond funds. Extended stretches of equity underperformance have proved to be great opportunities to buy stock funds for those investors who are patient and value-minded.

Making money in the stock market often involves making the right call about what's about to happen. No one can know the future, but what if you had a way to identify stocks that are on the way up before they attract a lot of attention? The fundamentalists, who tend to invest for the long term in stock funds, believe that undervalued stock funds are most likely to go up in price over time. They also believe that funds with consistent and solid growth rates are primarily comprised of, or include, low-risk stocks. Others who tend to invest for the short term look for evidence such as price movement to the upside.

Both of these schools of thought have merit. Therefore, buy safe, undervalued stock funds, rising in price. Experience has shown that if you want to make money in both bull and bear markets you must let the trend be your friend. You must buy rising funds in a rising market and sell falling funds in a falling market.

Making Money in Stock Funds

Buy low and sell high. The key to making money in both stock and bond markets lies in mastering the fine art of buying low and selling high. This, of course, is a lot easier said than done. When it comes to stocks, most of us have been taught that a stock fund's price is low after it has fallen in price. So we bought stock funds that were going down in price, hoping they would turn around and start going up. Bitter experience taught us that this was a dangerous practice. You never knew how low it might go. So the alternative would to be to buy stock funds that were going up in price.

In a chaotic economy, it's better to invest in financially strong funds that offer the potential for stable and dependable growth. Will the economy ever rebound? According to bond traders, it has already begun to do so. You can determine that yourself by looking at the yield curve and rates that are being paid by short- and long-term bonds. Since longer-dated bonds typically pay more than short-term debt, the yield curve usually slopes upward.

We have all been told that stock funds are long-term investments that only fluctuate in value over the short term. However, the erratic market gyrations that have occurred over the last couple of years don't support this scenario. If you agree, there are steps you can take to limit losses in any stock fund you own. You have to be willing to exercise a stop-loss or will-sell price on any stock fund you buy.

Here's how it works. To keep the numbers simple, let's say you bought one share of XYZ Stock Fund for $100. At the time you bought it, you determined that the maximum loss you were willing to accept was 10 percent, or a stop-loss price of $90. You also determined that you wanted to make 20 percent, or a will-sell price of $120.

Sometime after you bought XYZ Stock Fund, it goes up $20 to $120 a share. At this point, you're happy and sell, realizing a 20 percent gain. If the price had gone in the other direction, you would have exercised your stop-loss scenario and sold at $90 to minimize your loss to 10 percent and any further losses that might have occurred.

Bond Fund Basics

Bonds are fancy IOUs. Companies and governments issue bonds to fund their day-to-day operations and to finance specific projects. When you buy a bond, you are loaning money for a certain period of time to the issuer, be it General Electric or Uncle Sam. In return, bondholders get back their loan amounts plus interest. Bond funds invest in many securities with different interest rates and coupon payments. The income received from the bonds is distributed monthly to shareholders' 401(k) plans, and the distribution varies as does the daily value of the fund.

Individual bonds and bond funds are vastly different entities. Individual bonds pay a fixed stream of income and return your principal on a specific date, called the maturity date. Bond funds invest in many bonds with different interest rates and maturity dates. The fund's value varies daily, and the income that's received from the bonds is distributed monthly to shareholders. This income varies month to month.

You don't need to be a credit expert to read the bond market's tea leaves. But it is helpful to brush up on basic concepts. The most important thing to remember: bond prices and yields move in opposite directions. So when the demand for bonds grows and prices rise, yields fall.

Bonds are often referred to as fixed-income securities because they can generate a steady income in a diversified portfolio. They tend to move in the opposite direction of stocks and are an important way to buffer a stock portfolio and at the same time let you earn compound interest. Safe but lower-yielding bonds include Treasury bonds, investment-grade corporate bonds, municipal bonds, and bonds issued by government-sponsored agencies such as Fannie Mae. Riskier, higher-yielding bonds include corporate bonds that are rated below investment grade, also known as junk bonds.

Bond funds rely on their credit research departments to analyze an issuer's credit risk. Most investors don't have this knowledge or background to assess bonds. When buying a bond fund, always know exactly what you own, including the maturity date and the interest rate. Individual bonds or bond funds can be a good investment. But which way is right for you depends on your own needs, your risk tolerance, the time you have for research, and the amount of research you're prepared to do.

Why Invest in Bond Funds?

When it comes time to plotting investment strategy, you probably focus most of your attention on how equities are doing and pay scant attention to the inner workings of bonds. But as a word of caution, don't ignore the potential benefits of the fixed-income market. Trends in bond yields will often give you a better sense of the risks in the economy and your portfolio than stock funds can. Why? Equity investors are owners who care mostly about the upside potential of their holdings. Bond investors, by contrast, are creditors. They're worried about anything that could prevent them from getting their money paid back. So fixed-income investors are far more attuned to the current and near-term risks in the economy.

Bond funds are an excellent way to diversify your 401(k) plan with less money than what it costs to buy individual bonds. With whatever you want to spend, you can buy shares in a bond fund instead of spending a thousand dollars to buy one corporate bond. Bond funds often hold bonds from hundreds of companies, so you're shielded if a few companies default. By contrast, your returns suffer if you own a limited number of individual bonds from a handful of companies and an issuer defaults. With bond funds, you also get liquidity. You can sell fund shares any time at the fund's current value. Selling an individual bond often is tougher, if you must sell before maturity. They trade less frequently than stocks, and bonds typically trade "over the counter," meaning a broker hooks up buyers and sellers who negotiate price. Riskier bonds can be harder, and thus costlier, to unload.

Interest payments on bonds are usually fixed; thus bond funds are known as "fixed-income" investments. Bond prices move in the opposite direction of interest rates. When interest rates fall, bond and bond fund prices rise, and vice versa. If you hold a bond to maturity, price fluctuations don't matter. You will get back the original face value of the bond, along with all the interest you expect.

Making Money in Bond Funds

Since 1926 stocks of large companies have posted compound annual returns of around 10 percent versus 6 percent for long-term U.S. government bonds. Yet while stocks have returned more than bonds, they are also more volatile. Combining stocks with bonds gives a more stable portfolio. As seen during the bear market, the positive returns from bonds offset the double-digit losses from stocks.

Bonds can provide a worry-free stream of income. Handled with care, bond funds are among the most valuable tools in your 401(k) plan. However, don't invest all your retirement money in bonds. Inflation erodes the value of bonds' fixed interest payments. Stock returns, by contrast, stand a better chance of outpacing inflation. Despite the hammering stocks sometimes take, young and middle-aged people should put a large chunk of their money in stocks. Even retirees should own some stocks, given that people are living longer than they used to.

Investing in Government-Backed Bonds

United States Treasury bonds are the safest bonds of all because the interest and principal payments are guaranteed by the "full faith and credit" of the U.S. government. Because of their almost total lack of default risk, Treasury bonds carry some of the lowest yields around. When you do take money out of your 401(k) plan, the interest from bonds is exempt from state and local taxes, but not from federal tax. Treasury bonds offer various maturity dates. The features of specific government-backed bonds are summarized as follows:

◆ **U.S. Treasury Bonds.** Interest is exempt from state and local taxes, but not from federal tax when you take money out of your 401(k) plan. Because of their almost total lack of default risk, Treasury bonds carry some of the lowest yields around and offer different maturity dates.

- **Treasury Bills.** Treasury bills, or "T-bills," have the shortest maturities—thirteen weeks, twenty-six weeks, and one year. You buy them at a discount to their $10,000 face value and receive the full $10,000 at maturity. The difference reflects the interest you earn.

- **Treasury Notes.** Treasury notes mature in two to ten years. Interest is paid semiannually at a fixed rate. The minimum investment is $1,000 or $5,000, depending on maturity.

- **Treasury Bonds.** At ten years, Treasury bonds have the longest maturities. As with Treasury notes, they pay interest semiannually, and they are sold in denominations of $1,000.

- **Zero-Coupon Bonds.** Also known as "strips" or "zeros," zero-coupon bonds are Treasury-based securities that are sold by brokers at a deep discount and redeemed at full face value when they mature in six months to thirty years. Although you don't actually receive the interest until the bond matures, you must pay taxes each year on the "phantom interest" that you earn (it's based on the bond's market value, which usually rises steadily during the time you hold it). For that reason, these bonds are best held in tax-deferred accounts.

- **Inflation-Indexed Treasury Bonds.** Inflation-indexed Treasury bonds pay a real rate of interest on a principal amount that rises or falls with the Consumer Price Index.

You don't collect the inflation adjustment to your principal until the bond matures or you sell it, but you owe federal income tax on that phantom amount each year—in addition to tax on the interest you receive currently. Like zeros, these bonds are best held in tax-deferred accounts.

Investing in Treasury Bonds

One of the important lessons from the past few years is that stocks aren't everything. Although Treasury bonds have limited potential for serious appreciation, if well chosen, they can provide a steady flow of cash. (See Table 6.1.) I have traditionally recommended almost-no-risk Treasury bonds over corporate bond funds. High-quality corporate bond funds have returned only a half percentage

TABLE 6.1 ◆ Annualized return of Treasuries, 1926 to 2010

Period	Medium-Term Treasuries	Long-Term Treasuries
1 Year	5.5%	7.5%
5 Years	5.1%	7.1%
10 Years	6.0%	7.6%
20 Years	6.8%	8.6%
30 Years	8.3%	9.5%
40 Years	8.0%	8.5%
Average Return	5.3%	5.5%

Source: *Kiplinger Personal Finance, 10/2009*

point more than Treasury bonds. If you decide to invest in a bond fund, make sure that it has historically returned at least a percentage point higher than Treasuries.

The U.S. Treasury has a program that allows you to buy bonds directly from Uncle Sam. Municipal bond issuers such as states and cities offer "retail order periods" that allow individuals to buy their bonds directly. Some brokerage firms like Fidelity Investments allow you to buy bonds directly from certain companies.

Municipal bonds are one of America's favorite tax shelters. They are issued by state and local governments and agencies, usually in denominations of $5,000 and up, and mature in one to thirty or forty years. Interest is exempt from federal taxes, and if you live in the state issuing the bond, state and possibly local taxes as well. (Note that there are exceptions.) The capital gain you may make if you sell a bond for more than it cost you is just as taxable as any other gain; the tax exemption applies only to your bond's interest. Municipal bonds generally offer lower yields than taxable bonds of similar duration and quality. Because of their tax advantages, though, their after-tax returns are often higher than equivalent taxable bonds for people in the 28 percent federal tax bracket or higher.

Where to Find Quality Funds

Money magazine offers Money 70, shown in Figure 6.1, on the CNN website at money.cnn.com. (Select Personal

FIGURE 6.1 ◆ Money 70 mutual fund guide

| Home | Business News | Markets | Personal Finance | Retirement | Technology | Luxury | Small Bu |

| Retirement | Funds | Job search | ETFs | Loan Center | The Help Desk | College |

Living on Chinese stocks

10:47am: Marty Whitman of the Third Avenue Value Fund is hunting for deep values - and he sees them in Hong Kong. More

• Fund winners and fund losers

A fund battles back: up 45% this year

Oct 1: After a disastrous 2008, Longleaf Partners Fund is on the road to recovery, doubling down on some holdings and adding insurance to the mix. More

What you can learn from a closed fund

Sep 30: Vanguard's Primecap Core is no longer open to investors, but you can still poach a few ideas for your own portfolio. More

Hunting for bargain-bin value stocks

Sep 29: Fairholme Fund manager Bruce Berkowitz is going on the offensive and buying up value stocks that he says are ready to bounce back. More

MORE FUNDS NEWS

• ▶ Simple advice from a stock veteran
• Funds that are way up: Osterweis
• Strategies for a slow-go market
• Investing in the 'new normal'
• What's next? Ask the bond market
• Fidelity Contrafund open for business
• Nothing absolute about 'absolute return' funds
• Adventurous mutual funds for uncertain times
• Sweetening the dividend deal
• Make fear and greed work for you

ALL FUNDS NEWS

ULTIMATE MUTUAL FUND GUIDE

Money 70: Best funds in every category

Don't dwell on your losses. Focus on things you can control, like investing costs and consistency. That's what the Money 70 will help you do. More

ASK THE EXPERT

Recoup your bear market losses

There's a chance - even if you're in your late fifties. But you have to keep investing in stocks. More

Finance at the top of the main menu, and then select Mutual Funds to get to Money 70.) It lists the best funds by every category imaginable. Using Money 70, you can narrow down hundreds of funds to just a few that offer low fees and perform well, making your choice easier. It'll display a mix of high-quality funds that rank in the top half of their peers over five years that you can use to build a diversified portfolio. When it comes to actively managed funds, *Money* also looks for funds that have consistent strategies and superb management experience. *Money*'s site also checks Morningstar's stewardship fund rating grades, which rates such factors as a fund group's culture and regulatory history.

Balanced funds combine equity stakes with bond components, making them a good mix for conservative investors. Balanced funds number in the thousands, but only a few make the cut when they're narrowing down the possible Money 70 candidates based on their fees and performance. The concept behind these funds is simple. The equity portion is usually around 60 percent of assets, which gives shareholders a way to participate in any rally without the risk of an all-stock or all-bond portfolio. Balanced offerings will typically lag behind all-stock funds, but when the market reverses course, the bonds help cushion the blow by producing returns that beat their competitors.

Don't just pick a fund that has recently performed well. Look for funds that have performed well over the last two or three years and that are also rated "high" by Morningstar (morningstar.com), one of the premiere mutual fund rating companies in the country. Funds are rated with one to five stars, with one star as the lowest rating and five stars as the highest.

When evaluating funds, avoid those that have annual expense ratios greater than 1.5 percent of the fund's total assets.

Applying What You've Learned

- Develop your own buying and selling strategies for stock and bond funds. The primary way to outperform the market is to take more risks investing in stock funds. If you can't handle the risks in a shaky stock market, buy high-grade bond funds.

- Be patient. Take whatever time is necessary to get all of the information you need to make a buying decision. But also know when to be impatient. Set a stop-loss price for every fund you buy, and stick to it. Dump it if it's not performing.

- Don't avoid stocks. Despite the economy, people in their twenties, forties, and even seventies still should put a large chunk of their money in stock funds because of their higher returns.

- Do your research and decide which type and mix of bonds is right for your situation and financial goals.

CHAPTER 7

Investing in Index Funds

WITH A MIND-BOGGLING array of mutual funds to choose from, it's no wonder millions of Americans throw up their hands and surrender management of their finances to brokers, financial planners, and other advisors. That's a shame because you don't have to be a rocket scientist to pick funds astutely. By investing in index funds on your own, you can save a substantial amount of money not paying sales commissions to a broker or a percentage of your assets to an advisor for something you can do yourself.

The art of finding a quality index fund used to be relatively simple because when they were first introduced in the mid-1990s, there were only a few to choose from. Then Wall Street started muddying the waters. Over the past couple of years, hundreds of new index funds have been rolled out, encouraging naive investors to buy the most speculative "can't lose" funds. The steps covered in this chapter will help you find and invest in quality index funds if you approach your selection rationally and ignore Wall Street's hype.

Index Fund Basics

Sick of the high expenses charged by mutual funds and burned by the industry's dismal returns, many 401(k) investors are investing in low-cost index funds. Index funds are a fixed market basket of stocks, bonds, and other securities that track the performance of a specific stock or bond index.

Index funds have several advantages over traditional funds. Most trade just like a stock where a commission is charged on each buy or sell trade, and they're typically cheaper to flip. They can be bought or sold at any time during a trading day. By comparison, traditional mutual funds can be bought or sold only once in a trading day by a broker at full brokerage commissions. In addition, you're often required to hold a traditional mutual fund for a stipulated period of time before you can sell it or you'll be subject to an early sales penalty.

Index funds were created twenty years ago when the American Stock Exchange launched a series of index funds that were given the nickname of SPDR after the spider. SPDR Gold Shares trades under the exchange symbol GLD and tracks the price of gold, whereas SPDR

Large Cap (ELG) tracks the price of large-cap stocks. For the next decade, index funds were used largely by institutions and wealthy individuals as a way to hedge the market. After the mutual fund scandal erupted in 2003, retail investors started dumping their mutual funds and replaced them with index funds. Today, if your 401(k) plan doesn't offer index fund investment options, then ask your plan's administrator at work why it doesn't.

Index fund investments can offer wide diversification and are significantly cheaper than their actively managed mutual fund equivalents. Ideally, every 401(k) plan should be stuffed with low-cost index funds. If you have these options, your portfolio will likely perform better than 90 percent of the more expensive professionally managed funds.

Exchange Traded Fund Basics

Exchange traded funds (ETFs) are index funds that are easier to understand than their names suggest. Basically, ETFs are mutual funds that trade like stocks. Some copy the returns of broad stock and bond market indexes. Others replicate the performance of baskets of stocks in single industries or in niche investments, such as long-term growth ETFs like the Russell 3000 (IWV) designed for investors with a healthy tolerance for risk.

Growth and income ETFs like LQD generally buy high-quality U.S. corporate bonds, foreign government bonds (IGOV), and junk bonds (HDY). Foreign market ETFs, like EFA and DWX, generally invest in countries that have faster-growing economies than the U.S. economy, allowing you to diversify your investment in different currencies. Because of their low fees, ETFs are a great way to invest in bonds (PCY and LOD) and commodities such as energy (DBE), gold (GLD), and agricultural products (DBA).

Vanguard offers three index funds that illustrate what you should be looking for. Their total stock market index fund (VTSMX) contains large, medium, and small companies, mostly in the United States. Their international stock fund (VGTSX) covers large, medium, and small international companies. They also have a bond index fund (VBMFX) that invests in high-quality domestic bonds. For more information about Vanguard's index funds, visit vanguard.com. For more information on ETFs, visit amex.com, nyse.com, or nasdaq.com. To compare funds by cost, use the Mutual Fund Expense Analyzer at nasd.com.

Target-Date Index Fund Basics

Target-date index funds invest in other equities and follow an asset allocation that's suitable for investors with particular retirement time frames. The very name reflects the target date that the fund's asset allocation represents, like Retirement Plan 2020, which would have an allocation targeted toward investors retiring in 2020. As 2020 approaches, the fund's managers adjust the assets in the plan from high-risk investments like stocks to low-risk investments like Treasury bonds. If you decide to stay with the fund after you retire, the managers continue to reduce the investment risk to a more conservative portfolio. Target-date index funds are popular choices in 401(k) plans because they take the guesswork out of picking and allocating your own investments.

You can also use target-date index funds tailored to match your risk tolerance instead of your target retirement date. For example, if your target retirement date is 2030, but you would like to be more aggressive in your investments, you could use the 2040 fund. Conversely, if you want to be more conservative, you could use the 2020 fund. Some mutual fund companies offer lifestyle funds that are similar to target-date funds but cater to your level of risk (e.g., conservative, moderate, or high). Compare the funds of several companies before deciding which one(s) to invest in.

On the intermediate-maturity side, the Intermediate-Term Government Index has essentially the same maturity as Vanguard Intermediate-Term Treasury (VFITX). This index did exceptionally well during the recent market crisis, suffering just a 3.1 percent loss versus the Treasury fund's 3.4 percent loss.

On the long-term side, the new Long-Term Government Index and Long-Term Corporate Index hold fairly long bonds relative to the existing Vanguard funds. It's a testament to great management to see how well Vanguard Long-Term Investment-Grade Fund (VWESX) held up relative to the corporate index, generating better than average returns and smaller losses.

Why Invest in Index Funds?

For the most safety, go with index funds that track the major asset classes and come from a provider with a long, stable history like Vanguard. You can build a portfolio with just four or five index funds that will give you plenty of diversification. They're a great way to build a portfolio that matches your investment style. For example, you can construct an aggressive portfolio made up solely of stock ETFs. Or if you prefer a balanced approach, you can mix stock and bond funds. You can also use ETFs as an inexpensive way to boost your exposure to, say, fast-growing companies or emerging markets.

How to Find Quality Funds

Since there are so many index funds, it may make sense to focus on a smaller, more manageable portfolio of indexed ETFs. Determine what your objective is in investing in index funds. What are you trying to accomplish? For example, are you looking for maximum gains, and are you willing to accept the higher risks that come with lofty aspirations? If so, you might want a fund that buys shares of small companies or one that focuses on emerging markets, such as China and India. Or do you want steady income? That probably means you want a bond fund. If so, are you willing to settle for a fairly low yield to keep your risk down? Or are you willing to take on extra risk in search of high income? If the latter, consider a fund that invests in high-yield debt, also known as junk bonds.

Hone in on a specific fund category because the index fund world is a big place. It contains stock funds, bond funds, money market funds, and hybrids, which may own stocks, bonds, Treasury bills, and sometimes even commodities. And there are a myriad of choices within each broad category. Some funds, for example, invest in big companies while others invest in small or medium-size companies. Funds that invest in rapidly growing companies with high-priced stocks are different from those that care less about a company's growth prospects and more about buying its stock at a bargain price.

Consider the risk you're willing to take. Don't view "risk" as a four-letter word because there's nothing wrong with investing in risky funds. You'll need to assume some risk to achieve healthy gains. What's important is that you understand a fund's risk and can handle—both financially and emotionally—any potential losses. The Mutual Fund 2007 table on *Money* magazine's website (Money.com) provides insights about a fund's level of risk.

Funds are assigned a volatility ranking in the table, which measures the swings in a fund's returns. Volatility is great when funds are rising in value, but volatile funds tend to suffer the most during inhospitable markets or when their managers simply make bad decisions. The volatility rankings compare similar stock funds against each other.

Size up the funds that interest you. Bigger can be better, but it can also be a hindrance to good results in the future. Expenses at bigger funds are often significantly lower than those of smaller funds. That's a plus. But if a fund grows too big, it can become too unwieldy to manage effectively. In particular, the mere act of buying or selling stocks in vast quantities can move prices in an unfavorable direction.

There are no firm rules about what constitutes a fund that's too big. Much depends on the kinds of stocks a fund owns. In general, be wary of a fund that invests in large companies if its assets exceed $30 billion, particularly if the fund trades a lot. *Kiplinger* magazine's website (Kiplinger.com) features more than three thousand funds that you can review at your leisure. To make the job easier, you can see which funds are the top 25 performers over one-, three-, and five-year periods. The website groups the funds into more than thirty fund categories and updates them monthly, so you only need to select the categories that are of interest to you. To see the fund rankings, go to kiplinger.com/links/mutualfunds. Select Tools, and then click on Kiplinger's Fund Finder. (See Figures 7.1 and 7.2.)

FIGURE 7.1 ◆ Kiplinger fund finder

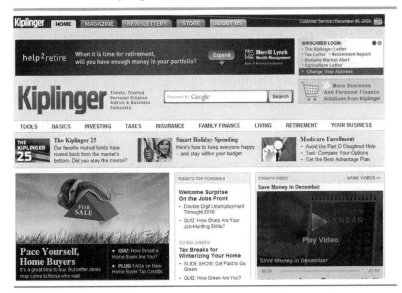

FIGURE 7.2 ◆ Kiplinger fund rankings

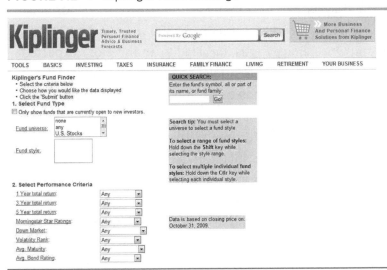

Automatic Investing in Funds

Automatic investing in index funds, such as monthly, is an option you may want to consider if your 401(k) plan offers it. Or, you can accumulate cash in your money market fund for investing in index funds periodically. It's a good idea to compare fees and rules at each company. Fidelity Investments, for instance, waives minimum investments in funds for participants in its automatic asset-builder plan, but not all companies do. T. Rowe Price does require a $50 minimum monthly deposit.

While ETFs don't carry the minimum investment limits that traditional funds generally do, brokerages often charge a transaction fee for every investment. American Century Investments allows automatic transfers and investments of as little as $50 as long as they total at least $600 a year. But the initial minimum investment for most American Century funds is $2,500. For its Live Strong and One Choice funds, targeted to an investor's expected retirement date or risk tolerance, the minimum is $500 as long as the customer transfers at least $100 a month to the account.

Fidelity waives minimum investments on many of its funds for automatic investors but requires transfers of at least $100. The transfers can be monthly, quarterly, or on a more customized schedule. There are no fees for transfers to a Fidelity account, but investing in some non-Fidelity funds costs $5 per transaction. The usual transaction fee for buying those funds online is $75, according to the Fidelity fee schedule.

Expense Ratios and Fees

Annual management fees for an index fund are expressed in a figure known as the expense ratio, which can vary widely. Those that track broad U.S. indexes usually charge less than 0.1 percent year, those that follow quantitative strategies run around 0.7 percent, and leveraged funds charge more, so shop around. After all, the low-cost advantage is one of the key reasons to buy index funds in the first place.

A lot of index funds claim to follow indexes but don't track established benchmarks such as Standard & Poor's 500 Index. Many of these offerings follow stock-picking approaches based on fundamentals, such as low price/earnings ratios or strong balance sheets. Such quantitative strategies may make sense, but they won't accurately mirror a broad asset class, so they pose a greater risk of underperforming the market.

Some index funds track narrow and exotic markets like crude oil or Colombian stocks. Since they often fail to attract enough investors, many close down. You will usually get your money back when an index fund closes. So unless you really want to speculate with your 401(k) money, shun funds that follow a narrow strategy and make sure any ETF you buy has accumulated assets of at least $50 million. Obscure ETFs may be costly to trade, as those that focus on narrow sectors and industries are often lightly traded. Such relative unpopularity can lead to spreads as wide as 50 cents between the "bid price" a buyer is ready to pay and the "ask price" a seller is ready to accept.

Watch your costs because fund fees can be confusing. To make matters as simple as possible, divide costs into two areas: fees you pay every year and charges—such as commissions—that you incur when you buy or sell a fund. Most commissions go to your 401(k) plan's provider.

Why get hung up on fees when plenty of funds with high fees have delivered good returns? We'll answer that question with another question: Why start investing with two strikes against you? If you pay a commission, you start the performance derby in the hole to the tune of the charge. And annual fees lower a fund's total return, whether it performs well or not. Because future performance is uncertain, it's best to avoid commissions and to invest in funds with below-average fees.

Study past performance. If past performance doesn't necessarily predict future results, why bother looking at a fund's record? The answer is that long-term results show whether a fund is well managed or not. You should look back at least five years, if possible, to gauge its performance.

Finally, check up on your funds periodically to see how they are doing. Go to fundalarm.com to see you if own any bad apples.

Applying What You've Learned

◆ Index funds are a fixed market basket of stocks, bonds, and other securities that track a benchmark. An ETF is an index fund that trades just like a stock where a commission is charged on each trade.

◆ Target-date index funds, as their name suggests, invest in equities and follow an asset allocation that's suitable for investors with a particular retirement time frame or "target date."

◆ Index funds track the major asset groups such as large-cap or small-cap stocks. If you invest in one, make sure they come from a provider with a long, stable history like Vanguard. Use them to help you build a diversified portfolio.

◆ The index fund world is made up of hundreds of stock funds, bond funds, international funds, commodities, and hybrids, so focus on or narrow in on a specific category of funds.

MANAGING YOUR RETIREMENT

I f you're getting ready to transition out of your job and into retirement, there are a number of things to consider. Our focus in Part 3 is to help you take the final steps to an exciting phase of your life, retirement. If you are already retired, then the chapters here will help you adjust your lifestyle as you migrate through a successful retirement for the rest of your life.

CHAPTER 8

Getting Ready to Retire

IF YOU'RE THINKING about retiring in the near future, you are bound to encounter some sleepless nights wondering whether or not you'll have enough money to live on for the rest of your life. Will you be able to invest your money wisely so that it will continue to grow? Are you ready to retire, and can you afford it? The following questionnaire will help you answer these important questions.

1. Have you developed a solid set of retirement goals that you have either met or are in the process of meeting?

2. Do you know how much money you'll need to support a retirement lifestyle that's acceptable to you?

3. Have you identified the sources of retirement income that you expect to receive after you retire?

4. Do you have any dependents that you must take care of after you retire? If yes, how will you handle this?

5. If you retire before you are eligible for Medicare (age sixty-five), do you have medical insurance to cover yourself?

One of the biggest fears people have when it comes to retirement is financial. According to *Forbes*, most retirees fail to meet their monthly expenses within the first year after they retire. That's because they didn't have a plan with specific goals before they retired. Be careful not to fall into the same trap.

You can head off the biggest fear by saving enough money to retire comfortably. Make sure you get a copy of my book, *The 250 Retirement Questions Everyone Should Ask*. It's available at Amazon (amazon.com), Barnes & Noble's website (barnesandnoble.com), and Borders' website (borders.com), among others. Charles Schwab's website will help you develop a retirement-ready plan with their online calculators. Go to their home page at schwab.com and click on Advice & Retirement at the top of the page.

What to Do Right Away

If you're fortunate enough to have a pension plan at work, make sure you know how much money you'll get, when you'll get it, and what your options are before you retire.

Lump-sum distribution options allow you to receive a one-time lump-sum distribution that you can either spend as you see fit or roll over into an IRA.

Now is the time to ease back on any risky investments that you might have in your portfolio. Take a look at your investments to see if they still meet your total needs and tolerance for risk. A good website for this is riskgrades .com. Trim anything that is too high a percentage of your total portfolio—more than 10 percent of a single stock or 20 percent of a fund, unless it is a broad index like Vanguard's total stock market fund (VTSMX) or bond fund like Harbor bond fund (HABDX). While you're taking inventory of your holdings, see if each of your investments is giving you a decent rate of return. If it's not meeting your expectations, get rid of it and replace it with a more promising investment.

Dollar cost averaging is a sane strategy to build your investment holdings. Decide how much you plan to invest each month or quarter after you retire. Pick a fund or several and arrange for a direct transfer of a fixed dollar amount out of your 401(k) cash account into the fund(s). Because your transfers are automatic, you're protected from letting your emotions or the latest news lead you to not invest. Plus, using the dollar cost averaging method, you will buy more shares when the price is lower and fewer shares when the price is high.

Managing a proliferation of investments can be challenging. If you can consolidate your investments into as few separate accounts as possible, it will simplify the management task. For example, consolidate previous employer retirement plans into a single IRA account or your current 401(k) plan. Use one brokerage firm instead of multiple banks or mutual fund companies to reduce the number of accounts you have to keep track of. With a single brokerage account, you can still follow each investment you own.

Another option is to use an online account consolidator tool like the one that's available for free at yodlee .com to help you keep track of multiple accounts, even if they are at separate financial institutions. When you link your accounts to the consolidator, it copies the information from the individual sites and presents it as a list on a single password-protected Web page.

Decide When to Activate Social Security

Social Security taxes are withheld from your paycheck on your first $102,000 of earning by 2010 rules. Your retirement benefits that you'll collect are based on how much you pay into the system while you are working. Your Social Security income can increase each year if the Consumer Price Index (CPI), which tracks the prices of most goods and services, goes up.

Unfortunately, the number of retirees eligible for Social Security is increasing compared to the number of workers who are paying into the system. You can expect the

Social Security Administration to compensate for this shift by lowering future benefits and extending the eligibility age for benefits. If this action is taken, you will have to rely more on your own saving for retirement security. The recession has brought the Social Security crisis even closer. The recent rise in unemployment translates into a sharp drop in payroll contributions. The problem of the future is now in the present.

The 2009 Social Security trustees' report shows that by 2016, tax revenues flowing into Social Security will be less than the benefits paid out. By 2037, the program's trust fund will be depleted. The bottom line is you can expect a number of changes will be made to the program as lawmakers attempt to resolve the program's pending deficit problems.

Deciding when to take your Social Security benefit is an important part of your retirement program and your long-term financial security. Currently, you can draw reduced benefits from the program at age 62 and full benefits at 65 if you were born before 1937. The age limit gradually creeps up to 67 if you were born after that time. Given the problems covered in the trustees' report, expect these age limits to continue to move up. To get the latest information, check out socialsecurity.gov/estimator to calculate an estimate of your benefit, or contact your local Social Security office at least six months before you want benefits to start. The office can also be contacted online at SSA.gov.

If you decide to take your benefit before you quit work-ing, there are limits on how much work income you can earn without a penalty. At present, you're required to give back $1 for every $2 you earn over the earnings limit. Check with Social Security at socialsecurity.gov to find out what the current limits are.

If you're not working, drawing benefits early can be advantageous. Although your monthly benefit will be lower than if you waited, if it helps reduce your need to withdraw money from your 401(k), it may make sense. On the other hand, if you're in good health and think you will live past the break-even age, you are probably better off waiting until you're eligible to receive the full benefit. The break-even age calculator on the Social Secu-rity website will help you estimate the age you need to live to in order to benefit from waiting to draw on Social Security.

If you are married, make sure you check on the effect your death has on your spouse's survivor benefit. A wid-owed spouse receives a part of the deceased spouse's ben-efit added to his or her Social Security benefit.

Sign Up for Medicare

Unfortunately, health costs generally increase as we get older. Make sure you know exactly what is and what is not covered—including prescription drugs—by Medicare or any private insurance you may have. Determine what your part is of any co-pay requirements. Typically, Medicare pays 80 percent and you pay 20 percent.

The financial crisis that Medicare faces is far greater than Social Security. Medicare's hospital insurance trust fund will be depleted by 2017. Since the late 1980s, the government budget has been combining the "actuarial surplus" in a Medicare fund. Thus, the current multi-trillion-dollar budget deficit is consuming almost every bit of that "surplus" that was supposed to be paying for medical care for baby boomers.

Regardless of when you decide to start taking Social Security benefits, you must apply for Medicare health insurance at age 65. Since aging baby boomers will put a strain on health insurance premiums including Medicare, you can expect health care costs to continue to go up annually. This can and probably will be a drain on your retirement savings. That drain combined with a lengthening life span for Americans demand that you consider all aspects of your personal health care in your retirement plan.

While there isn't anything you can do about increasing Medicare rates, some aspects of your health care are within your control. Maintaining a healthy weight by limiting the junk food you eat, exercising regularly, quitting smoking and drinking, and seeing your doctor at least once a year for an annual checkup are ways to reduce your risk of high medical costs in retirement.

Minimize Your Taxes

Don't assume that your taxes will be lower once you retire and stop earning taxable wages. This may not always be the case. Economists have consistently warned that tax rates may go up to cover the federal deficit. If your retirement accounts are invested in tax-deferred plans, then you'll owe income taxes on the withdrawals. If you elected to convert some or all of your tax-deferred plans to tax-free plans, then your tax liability will be less. A part of everyone's Social Security income is taxable, and withdrawals from most retirement plans are taxable as well. With the massive buildup of federal and some state budget deficits, tax rates could increase by the time you retire.

Should you pay taxes now or pay later? Taxes play a big part of retirement planning, particularly if you're nearing retirement. Arranging the investments in your retirement accounts to take advantage of the tax laws while you are working and after you retire is a consideration. Income and capital gains taxes will go up in the future to cover the multi-trillion dollar national deficit. Although you can't do anything about that, you can use the time you've got before you retire to take advantage of tax-saving options that are available to you. Make sure you know what income tax bracket you're in by visiting the IRS website at irs.gov. To help project your future taxes, use completetax.com.

Capital gains tax rates are lower than income tax rates and affect the stock part of your assets. Investments such as money market accounts and bond funds are mostly taxed at income tax rates and should be concentrated in tax-sheltered accounts like your 401(k). For example, if you've allocated 50 percent of your assets for retirement in stocks and 50 percent in bonds and money market accounts, ideally you would have most of your stocks in taxable accounts where you can take advantage of lower capital gains tax rates and the rest of your funds held in retirement accounts.

If you're thinking about relocating after you retire in the hopes of enjoying milder weather and lower expenses, make sure you first assess the overall tax burden of potential locations. Some states that are currently tax friendly could get a lot less tax friendly as they scramble to find new sources of revenue to plug gaping holes in their recession-shredded budgets.

Although federal taxes won't change, state and local taxes can vary significantly from one location to another. If you itemize deductions, how much you pay in local property taxes for the same house in different states can vary widely. *Where to Retire* magazine (wheretoretire .com) offers a state-by-state tax guide, including special exemptions for seniors and a rundown of how various types of retirement income are taxed. *Kiplinger* magazine offers an interactive retiree tax map on their website at kiplinger.com/links/retireetaxmap.

Estimate Your Cash Flow

Cash flow is an accounting exercise where you identify the sources of cash you've got coming in and how you plan to apply that cash to specific expenses. The techniques used to determine your cash flow are similar to the steps you went through to prepare a budget. Start by reviewing your regular monthly living expenses, like food, utilities, and mortgage payments, and periodic non-monthly payments like insurance premiums to determine how much cash is needed to cover those expenses.

The next step is to determine your non-monthly expenses, like property taxes, insurance payments, car maintenance, and travel, over the next twelve months. Then total these expenses and divide them by twelve to convert them to an estimated monthly expense. The final step in determining your cash flow is to find out what your monthly income will be from sources like Social Security and monthly pension payments. Table 8.1 shows what your retirement cash flow might look like.

The total of the monthly and non-monthly income needs to be more than the monthly expense and the non-monthly expense prorated to a monthly amount. That's

TABLE 8.1 ◆ Estimate of retirement cash flow

Income Expense Category	Example of Items Covered	Monthly $	Annual $
Monthly Income	Social Security, pension, 401(k) withdrawal	$5,000	$60,000
Non-Monthly Income	Tax refunds, personal loans	$0	$2,000
Subtotal		$5,000	$62,000
Monthly Expenses	Rent, mortgage payments, utilities, food, car-related expenses, credit cards, etc.	$4,500	$54,000
Non-Monthly Expenses	Property taxes, insurance premiums, medical bills, travel, etc.	$0	$7,000
Subtotal		$4,500	$61,000
	Total Cash Needed	$500 Surplus	$1,000 Surplus

because emergencies and unplanned expenses will occur after retirement just as when you were working. To keep these surprise expenses from draining your retirement accounts, put your surplus money in a savings account that you can draw on to cover unexpected expenses.

If you need to withdraw money from a retirement account like your 401(k), make sure it's an amount that you're comfortable with. For example, if you have $50,000 in your account and based on your total monthly expenses you need an additional $500 a month out of your 401(k) to cover your expenses, then you will be using up 1 percent of your 401(k) to meet your cash flow needs. That means that over the next 100 months (100 months × $500 = $50,000), your 401(k) will dwindle down to zero dollars. That assumption assumes that it's not invested in anything. However, if it is invested in assets that on average are realizing a compound annual interest rate of 12 percent, or $6,000 per year, then your 401(k) is meeting your cash flow needs without losing any value.

Reallocate Your Assets

If you bought your home years ago, chances are you've ended up with an asset that's worth more than you paid for it. And if you have paid off the mortgage, it could be the cornerstone of your retirement nest egg. The opportunity to leverage the equity you've built up is something you should think about. As you approach retirement, there are several options to consider when you evaluate whether you should keep or sell your home.

Consider trading down, particularly if you believe you won't need the size of home you're living in now when you retire. What will it cost to get an acceptable smaller replacement? If the potential profit from selling your home is minimal, it might not be worth the effort to sell it before you retire.

Time the sale of your home to take advantage of the tax breaks. If you or your spouse is 55 or older, you can exclude from taxes up to $500,000 of the capital gain on the sale of your home. You may want to consider selling your home and moving where the cost of housing and living are lower. Not only will you get more home for your money, you will get the added benefit of a lower cost of living.

Deal with Inflation

One of the reasons to have interest-bearing assets in your 401(k) plan is to make sure your retirement income keeps up with inflation. There are several steps you can take that will help you deal with inflation. Annually track your expenses in an online inflation calculator like those offered at mint.com or yodlee.com so that you can see how inflation is affecting you. Your personal inflation rate is the percentage your expenses increased over last year.

Fortunately, inflation has been relatively tame over the past decade. But, watch out because it could become a significant factor as we move into the second decade of this century. The huge accumulation of trillions of dollars in federal debt over the last couple of years is in and of itself inflationary. Government will have to either borrow more money to pay for the deficit or significantly increase taxes. If it takes the easy way out and borrows the money, that will drive up the cost of loans (i.e., interest rates) for everybody, including American businesses, which adds to their cost of producing the products and services we consume. Who's going to pay for it? You got it—the higher prices will be passed on to consumers.

And the resulting high inflation will be detrimental to the health of the economy, to say the least. It erodes the buying power of money, which is particularly bad for retirees on fixed incomes. Inflation is usually not a problem when the economy is weak, which is the one good thing about recessions. Retail spending plunges and unemployment is up, which takes pressure off prices. And, of course, increases in the price of oil are readily visible to you at the gas pump. Its inflationary impact immediately hits your pocketbook.

Price increases due to inflation should be taken into consideration when you calculate how much you'll need when you retire. The inflation rate is measured by the Consumer Price Index (CPI), which is reported on a regular basis in the financial sections of newspapers and on the news media. Pay close attention to the CPI because it's one way to gauge whether your living expenses might be going up or down. Increases in the costs of home maintenance and medical care, in particular, can adversely affect your retirement savings.

Make Hard Choices

Sometimes cutting back on what you're spending is all you need to do to get ready for retirement. If that doesn't make a big enough dent to help you make ends meet, you may need to look at some major items that are costing you the most money. You may have to make some hard choices now if you want to retire. If you haven't been able to bring your expenses in line with your retirement income, the question is not whether you are going to have to make hard choices, but rather which hard choices are you going to make.

Is your car sabotaging your ability to make ends meet? If so, do you really need it after you retire? In the interim, is there a cheaper way for you to get back and forth to work each day? There probably is if you think about it. If you're willing to get rid of your car, you could save hundreds of dollars on payments, upkeep, gasoline, and insurance. If you can't survive without a car, consider selling it and getting a cheaper one that will get you from point A to point B just fine, with less luxury.

If you have made it this far in this book and you still have no idea of what you need to do to get out of debt, consider getting help from a credit counselor. A credit counselor can put you in a debt management program if he or she is willing to accept you as a client. Your counselor will arrange for you to pay off your debts, usually at a lower interest rate. In exchange, you have to agree to stop using your credit cards and applying for additional credit. From this point, you make one payment (usually monthly) to your counselor, who in turn pays your creditors. If you break the agreement, you will be removed from the program. If you're interested in such a program, start your search for a counselor online at simpleliving.net or debtorsanonymous.org.

If your personal debt is escalating to the point where you're having trouble paying even the minimum on your debts and collecting agencies are hounding you, then you need to take some hard action right now because it probably won't get any better when you stop working and start living on your retirement income. You may want to consider declaring bankruptcy. If you need more information about bankruptcy, go to clearbankruptcy.com.

Applying What You've Learned

- If you're fortunate enough to have a pension plan at work, make sure you know how much money you'll get and when you'll get it.
- Ease back on any risky investments that you might have and review your portfolio to see if your investments still meet your total needs.
- Know when you want to take your Social Security, and remember you must apply for Medicare health insurance at age sixty-five.

- Don't assume that your taxes will be lower once you retire and stop earning taxable wages because that may not always be the case.
- Do a retirement cash flow assessment. The total of the monthly income needs to be more than monthly expenses and non-monthly expenses (prorated to a monthly amount) to be financially comfortable in retirement.
- Consider, if you have paid off the mortgage, leveraging the equity into a smaller home.
- Make some hard choices now, before you retire, if cutting back on what you're spending doesn't make a big enough dent to help you make ends meet.

CHAPTER 9

Making Your Money Last

LIFE IS FILLED with many significant transitions, and certainly your retirement counts as one of them. When you retire, the importance of managing your money takes on a whole new meaning. You're counting on the money in your 401(k) plan and other retirement accounts to financially carry you through for the rest of your life. That may raise several questions in your mind. Is your investment mix right for you when you retire? Would you be better off moving some of your speculative investments into more conservative, less risky investments? These issues and more are discussed in this chapter.

A Lifetime of Money

Once you have your Social Security strategy nailed down, there's just one little retirement question left to consider: How can you make the money that you've so diligently saved provide the life you want for as long as you live? Figuring out how to draw secure retirement income from a portfolio is a challenge in the best of times. Having seen the worst recession since the Great Depression unfold over the past few years, you've probably gone into loss-avoidance mode. But avoiding market risk leaves you vulnerable to inflation and the risk that you'll outlive your money. No one investment can protect you from every risk you'll face, but hiding in cash will probably not see you through your retirement years. What you need is a basket of investments that provides:

- stable income you're not likely to outlive
- the potential for that income to grow ahead of inflation
- the ability to access cash to meet unexpected needs
- adequate protection from market downturns

An important part of protecting your money is to have enough set aside to take care of unplanned expenses like car repairs without having to take money out of your retirement account. Keep some cash on hand to cover emergency expenses. If you find yourself tempted to spend on unneeded items, ask yourself if you really need them. Just say no, and instead, put the money in your emergency savings account. Many people who are hard-pressed to save find it relatively easy to come up with the money to buy things they want but don't need. Wants are things that might make life a little more fun in the short term, but that's it.

Think of your emergency savings as a way to pay for what you need, not want, to maintain your healthy lifestyle. Make sure you leave room in your cash reserves for big-ticket items like your car. How long will your current car last? Will you have to replace it with a new one, or can you get by with a cheaper used car? Will you have to replace some of your home furnishings? Will maintenance on your home be required? Can you make the repairs yourself? These are just some of the questions you need to ask yourself. When you project your monthly and annual expenses, consider the average cost of these and other unplanned expenses and include an estimated dollar amount to cover them.

Check Your Investment Mix Appreciation

Ensuring that you have a mix of investments that are appreciating in value is an important part of having a retirement plan. The mix in your portfolio will change as you get older. It's based on the eventual results you're looking for and your time frame. You periodically adjust it to suit the amount of risk you're willing to take. Deciding on what's the right mix for you is a relatively simple task once you know how it's done and what's involved. For example, you don't want a portfolio that is too risky or one that's not aggressive enough to grow.

There are two important reasons to have an asset allocation plan. First, it is easier to predict the future performance of your overall portfolio by studying the historical performance of the mix and the current news that may be affecting the mix. The second reason for the mix is that it ensures that you own a variety of investment categories. The idea behind diversification is to reduce risk while increasing your expected returns. If one of your selections is going down, others are hopefully going up to offset it.

Each investment category (stock funds, bond funds, and so on) is influenced by different market and economic factors. Stocks typically do better during one part of the market cycle, while bonds do better in another. This balancing is why your allocation plan is so important. If you understand how basic market factors affect your mix of investments, you are in a better position to reallocate your assets in response to the ups and downs of the market.

For example, let's assume you're comfortable with accepting some risk in your portfolio and have selected a mix of 75 percent stocks and 25 percent bonds. Market forces begin to favor bond returns and are driving stock prices down. You rebalance your portfolio mix by selling some of your stock funds to buy bond funds to obtain a 50/50 percentage allocation mix. When the situation reverses itself and the economic forces begin to favor stocks, you sell some of your bond holdings at a profit and buy cheap stocks that are on their way up. By periodically rebalancing your mix whenever the economy dictates, you will be buying investments at low prices and selling at high prices.

Managing a mix of investments on a recurring basis gives you an opportunity to rebalance your portfolio, improving the mix. For example, you may decide to sell assets that have done well and use the cash to buy other investments that are trading at low prices. Two of the best online asset allocation tools are dinkytown.com and calc xml.com. Both help you determine an investment mix based on your time horizon and tolerance for risk. There is an online asset allocation questionnaire, available at smartinvestmentbook.com, that will help guide you to proper asset allocation for your retirement portfolio.

Asset Alternatives

The following sections describe asset alternatives for three different retirement situations. The first assumes that you will have enough cash when you retire to meet your monthly living expenses. The second assumes that you have almost enough cash, and the third assumes you don't have enough cash to retire comfortably.

You Have Enough Money

If you expect to have enough income from Social Security, pensions, and retirement accounts to cover all of your basic monthly expenses, there are several asset allocation options that you may want to consider. The scenario that follows assumes you've built a diversified portfolio of stocks, bonds, and cash that has the potential to generate enough income to stay ahead of inflation. It also assumes that you believe you could weather a market downturn and are confident in your ability to manage your portfolio.

You withdraw money as needed to meet your retirement expenses, starting off with a 4 percent annual withdrawal—$20,000 on a $500,000 portfolio—and increase the dollar amount by the inflation rate each year. Done correctly, you will have an 80 percent chance of your money lasting thirty years. The higher the withdrawal rate, the lower your odds. So this option may not work if you need more income than 4 percent would provide or if you live longer than thirty years.

◆ **Possible Risks.** A sizable loss early in retirement could undo you. If your portfolio loses 20 percent the first year, the chances of your savings lasting thirty years will drop to roughly 50 percent. Alternatively, if the market does well over the long run, you could be left with a huge sum late in life, so you would have lived more frugally than you had to.

◆ **Offsetting Risks.** Asset allocation is a key to the security of your retirement money. Going 100 percent into bonds might protect you from a market meltdown, but you will probably lose out to inflation. Loading up on stocks gives you a better shot at increasing your income, yet you may get mauled by a bear market. So you might want to aim for the middle ground. For someone entering retirement, a broadly diversified 50/50 stock-to-bond blend is a reasonable starting point.

You also have to be flexible with withdrawals. In a declining market you may have to skip the inflation boost or scale back the amount you withdraw. Conversely, if the markets go on a run, you may be able to take out more. Finally, be strategic in the way you tap assets. Start with taxable accounts; then tax-deferred accounts, such as 401(k)s and traditional IRAs; and then tax-free IRAs. That way the latter accounts compound longer without the drag of taxes, so you can build bigger balances and draw more income over time.

You Almost Have Enough Money

This scenario may apply to you if you need more income for basic retirement expenses than you'll get from Social Security, pensions, and your retirement accounts. You'd like to avoid subjecting all your savings to market volatility. Consider investing a portion of your savings in a lifetime immediate annuity, an insurance product that will send you fixed monthly checks for as long as you and/ or your spouse live. That way, you'll have a layer of guaranteed income to help cover monthly expenses and still have funds in your retirement account that you can tap.

This option provides longer income security because the payout from an immediate annuity can't be easily matched by another sure-bet investment. Immediate annuities pay roughly 8 percent for a 65-year-old man, or about $40,000 a year on a $500,000 annuity. You'd have to invest significantly more to get the same assured lifetime income from long-term Treasuries. The reason immediate annuities pay so well is because your money is pooled with others', allowing insurers to essentially transfer funds from clients who die early to those who live past their life expectancies.

+ **Possible Risks.** Once you purchase an immediate annuity, you typically give up access to the money used for the purchase. You can't use it for a new roof or a vacation in France, and you can't pass it down to your kids. Plus, if you die early in retirement, the annuity will have paid out less than you put in. These are some of the reasons why many people perceive immediate annuities as potentially wasted money. Another concern is that annuity payments are usually fixed, which means they'll be worth less over time because of inflation. A few insurers offer inflation-adjusted immediate annuities, but the monthly payouts are considerably lower. While annuities eliminate market and longevity risks, your annuity income security is based on the financial health of the annuity provider.

◆ **Offsetting Risks.** In reality, money in an annuity is no more "wasted" than the premiums you pay to insure your car. So try to get over that psychological hurdle, since this option offers you a chance of maintaining the recurring income you need. To make it work, you want to devote enough to the annuity so that the income, along with Social Security, and pensions, will cover all your expenses. But don't go overboard with an annuity or you'll lose too much liquidity in what's left over in your retirement accounts.

There's no one "right" mix. Splitting savings 50/50 between an immediate annuity and a diversified portfolio can provide the same 4 percent inflation-adjusted income as was used in the first option—but with a 99 percent chance of lasting thirty years. If you can live with less certainty, you can boost your income to, say, 4.5 percent by drawing more from your portfolio. Or, you could invest less in the annuity. To mitigate the risk of an annuity provider going out of business, stick to companies that are highly rated by the two top corporate rating firms in the country, Standard & Poor's and A.M. Best. Check at nolhga.com that the amount you'll invest with a company is covered by your state's insurance guaranty association.

You Don't Have Enough Money

This scenario may apply to you if you need more income than Social Security, pensions, and your retirement account will provide. While maintaining a stock/bond portfolio, you may want to invest a portion of savings in an immediate annuity and a portion in a variable annuity with a guaranteed lifetime withdrawal benefit (GLWB). Such annuities allow you to choose limited investments, and you can withdraw funds when needed. Your variable annuity income has the potential to grow if your investments appreciate, making it more flexible than an immediate annuity.

For example, let's say you invest $250,000 in a variable annuity that guarantees 5 percent, or $12,500 a year. If, on your contract anniversary date, a rising market has pushed your balance to $300,000 after fees, your 5 percent will be applied to that amount, boosting your income to $15,000 a year. Even if a market crash later knocks your account to $200,000, you're still guaranteed $15,000.

♦ **Possible Risks.** Flexibility comes at a price. First, variable annuities pay significantly less than immediate annuities for the same amount invested. Second, the plans come with high fees, often 3 percent or more a year. That makes it difficult for your account value to grow and keep pace with inflation. Third, though you can draw more than your guaranteed amount from the account, doing so will reduce your income for future years.

♦ **Offsetting Risks.** The high fees and low payout of the variable annuity explain why you need an immediate annuity in the mix: without it, the odds of maintaining your target income are slightly lower than with a stock/ bond portfolio alone. Together you want the payouts, along with Social Security and pensions, to cover your basic expenses. The more you put in the variable annuity versus an immediate annuity, the more access you'll have to your retirement accounts.

In exchange, you'll settle for a lower guaranteed payout. A reasonable asset mix might be to put 25 percent of your money into an immediate annuity, 25 percent in a variable annuity, and the other 50 percent in stock and bond funds. That gives you a 90 percent chance of getting the income you will need for thirty years. You'll end up giving away more of your savings than with the other two strategies, but you have to pay for security one way or another.

Annuity Options

The word *annuitizes* means that you take a fixed sum of money and convert it into a series of regular payments. You can purchase an annuity from insurance companies and some brokerage firms. Payments are usually made monthly and are structured to continue on a particular schedule that could be for your lifetime or over a specified time period, like five years.

Installment payments are made for a set amount over a specified period of time such as five, ten, or fifteen years. A life annuity pays for as long as you live. Joint annuities pay you and another person (e.g., a spouse) through the end of the longer of the two lifetimes. Single-life annuities pay a stipulated amount on a regular basis (e.g., monthly) until you die. An annuity with spousal benefits pays a stipulated amount on a regular basis until you die and then pays your spouse a stipulated amount on a regular basis until he or she dies.

A recurring annuity pays you and your spouse a stipulated amount on a regular basis until you or your spouse dies and continues paying the same amount until the remaining spouse dies. Many 401(k) providers offer annuity options to participants in their plans, and most major life insurance companies offer annuity products.

Reverse Mortgage Options

On the surface, a reverse mortgage sounds like a "can't lose" deal for older homeowners who are about to retire. A lender gives you what amounts to a cash advance on your home equity, and you don't have to pay it back until you move or die. At that time, the lender sells the home and uses the proceeds from the sale of your home to close out the loan. Reverse mortgages are particularly appealing to retirees looking to supplement their limited retirement income. You have to be at least 62 to qualify for a reverse mortgage.

There are some serious drawbacks to reverse mortgages if it's an option that you're considering. You can expect to pay high fees to get a reverse mortgage. In addition to regular closing costs, you'll pay an origination fee of 2 percent or more on the first $200,000 of the loan and 1 percent or more thereafter. You'll also be required to pay a mortgage insurance premium of about 2 percent plus a monthly service charge as well. By the time you add all the fees together, they can easily reach $10,000 or more.

The formula for determining your loan amount takes into account your age and current interest rates as well as your home's value. Anything you owe on your home is subtracted from that amount, as are all loan fees. The older you are, the more you can borrow. To see how much you might qualify for, use the online calculator at revmort.com/nrmla.

Before you can get a reverse mortgage, you'll be required to attend a session with a financial counselor who is not affiliated with the lender. Before you sign up a counselor, make sure you understand all the risks that are involved with reverse mortgages. Look into all the alternatives you may have such as cutting expenses, taking out a home-equity line of credit, or downsizing your home.

Downsizing your house is a great way to free up some money instead of getting a reverse mortgage. If you don't plan to live in your current home when you retire, so much the better. Unmarried homeowners are allowed to realize $250,000 in capital gains when they sell their primary residence. If you're married, you get double that amount, or $500,000. You can then take your time to explore the places you might want to retire without have to commit to the expense of owning another home.

Returning to Work Options

Planning to work part-time after you retire is an option you might want to consider if you're concerned that you may not have saved enough for retirement. A retirement job may be a part-time version of your current job or something that you always wanted to do on your own. If you're thinking about ways to earn extra money after you retire, start thinking about it now, before you retire. That'll give you time to check out the viability of the options you're considering. Make sure you determine how much you might earn before you add the extra income to your retirement calculations.

Many Americans out of necessity start their own business before or after they retire. Unfortunately, of the more than 600,000 companies started in the United States each year, only about half survive the first five years. What steps can you take to make sure you're among the survivors? Start by creating a business plan that clearly identifies what you want to do, how much it will cost you to start the business up, and what you can expect to make. Is there a market for the products and services you want to offer? Before you start investing real money, focus your efforts on finding out everything you can about the business sector that's in your plan by analyzing competitors' pricing and marketing techniques. This will help you shape your ideas. If you need help, seek out your local Score office (sba.gov). Score is a nonprofit partner of the Small Business Administration that has more than eleven thousand counselors who mentor people on every aspect of starting a small business.

Applying What You've Learned

- ◆ To assure that you'll have enough money when you retire, you'll need a basket of investments that provide a stable income you're not likely to outlive and the potential for that income to grow ahead of inflation. Review the options available to help you meet that goal.
- ◆ Ensuring that you have a mix of investments that is appreciating in value is an important part of your retirement plan. The allocation of your assets will change as you get older.
- ◆ An annuity option annuitizes the money you pay for it and makes monthly payments to you over your lifetime or over a specified time period.

- With a reverse mortgage, a lender loans you a cash advance on your home equity, which you don't have to pay back until you move or die. At that time, the lender sells the home and uses the proceeds to close out the loan.
- There are other options to explore before resorting to a reverse mortgage, such as moving out of a larger home into one that's less expensive to free up some money.
- Planning to work part-time or starting your own home business after you retire is an option if you're concerned that you may not have saved enough for retirement.

CHAPTER 10

Setting Up
Your Estate Plan

IF YOU PLANNED it right, your retirement accounts will outlive you. This chapter explains how to create an estate plan so your heirs will receive as much of your hard-earned cash as possible. Don't ignore this chapter even if you're young, because the needs of your family are still there. There are special tax benefits within your retirement accounts that can be extended to your family. Making a will is not difficult, but it is undeniably a serious and sobering process.

What's an Estate Plan?

Your estate plan is the final component in your retirement plan. It's your assurance that everything you have worked for all your life will be distributed to your loved ones, according to your wishes.

An estate plan arranges for your assets to be distributed when you die or if you are incapacitated. It is an important way to make your wishes known regarding your finances and personal care. Most estate plans begin with a will, which, among other objectives, specifies what happens to your property when you die. A will combined with a living trust will allow you to spell out what you want under specific circumstances, for instance, if you need medical treatment. For example, you can specify whether you want life-support equipment under certain medical conditions so that your family members don't have to make that difficult decision of your behalf.

An estate plan can include:

- making arrangements for the care of your young children in the event of your death
- planning for your own care in case you can't make decisions on your own
- taking steps so that your inheritors can avoid probate court proceedings after your death
- planning to avoid federal or state estate tax, if you own a large amount of property

Everything that you own when you die—including your 401(k) and IRA—becomes part of your estate. And, if it's not left to your spouse, it could be taxed under the estate tax rules. Beneficiaries have immediate access to the retirement account(s) you leave with them, regard-less of their ages. If you manage your retirement accounts correctly, beneficiaries may be able to keep the money in your retirement accounts and enjoy the tax benefits.

The Difference Between Wills and Living Trusts

Both wills and living trusts let you leave your property to the people you want to inherit it. You can revoke or change a will or a trust at any time, for any reason, before you die. The major difference between them is that assets left in a living trust don't have to go through probate court proceedings at your death. That's because when you create a living trust, you transfer ownership of the designated property to yourself as "trustee" of the trust. During your lifetime, you still have control over all the property in your living trust and can do what you want with it—sell it, spend it, or give it away. Then, after your death, the person you named in the trust as trustee distributes the property to family members and friends as you specified.

A living trust involves more paperwork to create than a will because you must transfer ownership of the prop-erty to yourself as trustee and conduct future personal business in the name of the trust. But there is no need to file a separate tax return for the trust because all trans-actions, such as the sale of trust property at a profit, are reported on your personal income tax return. A trust also offers a way that the trust property can be taken care of if you become incapacitated and are unable to handle it yourself. The person you appointed in your trust to take over and manage your property does that for you. If you don't have a trust, close family members may have to go to court to get that kind of authority should you become incapacitated.

Many people create both a will and a living trust. It's common to use a living trust to leave some assets to heirs to avoid probate and leave the rest by will. In fact, even if you make a living trust, you'll still want to make a simple backup will to handle property you didn't get around to transferring to the trust. Table 10.1 includes some factors

TABLE 10.1 ♦ Wills versus living trusts

What Wills and Living Trusts Can Do	Will	Living Trust
Avoid probate		X
Reduce estate tax	X	
Keep your estate plan confidential		X
Set up management of property for minors	X	X
Arrange management of your property if you become incapacitated		X
Appoint a guardian to raise young children if you can't	X	

to think about when you're deciding whether the centerpiece of your estate plan should be a will or a living trust.

The larger your estate, the larger the potential probate cost and the less likely that your estate will qualify for simplified probate proceedings. Often it makes sense to making sure major assets, such as real estate or business assets, are transferred in a way that avoids probate. You don't need a trust to avoid probate for assets like your 401(k) and other retirement accounts. It's a matter of filling out simple beneficiary forms that your 401(k) provider can give you.

A will can do one important thing that a living trust can't. It allows you to name someone (called a personal guardian) to raise your minor children in the unlikely event that neither you nor the other parent is available. Caring for children if both parents die or are unavailable is an important concern for most parents. State succession laws do not specify who will take care of your children. So if you don't name a guardian in your will, it is left up to the courts and social service agencies to find and appoint a personal guardian.

Setting Up Wills and Living Trusts

Everybody should have a will and a living trust, whether you are single or married, young or old, healthy or sick. Making a will is the best way to leave property to family, friends, and organizations of your choice after your death. By creating both documents, you are assured that your hard-earned money stays in the family or goes to the people or organization of your choice. You designate someone whom you have confidence in such as your spouse or a sibling to act as your estate's executor. This person will be responsible for paying off your creditors and taxes and ultimately splitting your estate among your heirs in accordance to the wishes in your will.

To create a will, you must either be at least 18 years old or living in a state that permits people under 18 to create a will or trust. While this sounds like a subjective standard, the laws generally require that you must:

◆ know what a will and trust are and what they do before you create one or both
◆ be of sound mind to prepare a valid will and/or trust
◆ understand the relationship between you and the people who would normally be provided for in your will and trust, such as a spouse or children
◆ understand the kind and quantity of property you own, and be able to decide how to distribute your belongings

Individual state laws determine whether a will or trust made by a resident of the state is valid. If a will is valid in the state where it is made, it is valid in all other states. Contrary to what many people believe, a will or trust need not be notarized to be legally valid. But adding a notarized document verifying that it was signed and witnessed can be helpful when it comes time to file the will in probate court.

In most states, a will and trust must:

- include at least one substantive provision—either giving away some property or naming a guardian to care for minor children who are left without parents
- be signed and dated by the person making it and be witnessed by at least two other people who are not named to take property under the will
- be clear enough so that others can understand what the testator intended—nonsensical, legalistic language such as "I hereby give, bequeath, and devise" is both unwise and unnecessary

If you decide to create a will or trust, consider using an estate-planning attorney to help you draft the documents. You can draft one from do-it-yourself personal computer software like Quicken's Will Maker (quicken.com), but any saving you incur by not paying attorney fees is hardly worth the risk of a mistake or oversight on your part.

Preparing Your Own Will

As a way to distribute property, the will has been around in substantially the same form for about 150 years. Self-help was originally the rule and lawyer assistance the exception. During the Civil War, it was highly unusual for a person to hire a lawyer to formally set out what should be done with his or her property. However, in the past fifty years, the legal profession has scored a public relations coup by convincing many people that writing a will without a lawyer is like doing your own brain surgery and you could make costly mistakes. The hardest part of making a will is figuring out who will get your property when you die.

In about half the states, handwritten, or holographic, wills are legally valid. The most obvious problem with a holographic will is that after your death, it may be difficult to prove that your handwritten document was actually written by you and that you intended it to be your will. Only a few states accept oral wills under very limited circumstances, such as when a mortally injured person utters his or her last wishes. It is often difficult to prove the authenticity of an oral will. Handwritten wills or one that's prepared on your personal computer are fraught with possible legal problems as well. At a minimum, make sure you sign your will and have it notarized.

A properly signed and witnessed will is much less vulnerable to challenge by anyone claiming it was forged or fabricated. If need be, witnesses can later testify in court that the person whose name is on the will is the same person who signed it and that making the will was a voluntary and knowing act.

If you die without a valid will, money and other property you own at death will be divided and distributed to others according to your state's intestate succession laws. These laws divide all property among the relatives who are considered closest to you according to a set formula—which completely excludes friends and charities.

Selecting Beneficiaries

Typically one spouse names the other spouse as primary beneficiary. Then when the spouse dies, the children—if they are named as contingent beneficiaries—would inherit the estate. You can have more than one primary beneficiary. For example, if you designated your spouse as a primary beneficiary to inherit 75 percent and one of your kids to receive 25 percent, then you would have two primary beneficiaries. If you're not married, or do not have children, you would name other beneficiaries. You could also designate multiple contingent beneficiaries, each sharing whatever percentage you want.

You are allowed to name any beneficiary you want (i.e., person or organization) for a specified retirement account, and they get the money after you die. That's because retirement accounts are not controlled by the probate process and your will. If properly managed, this can work out great for your heirs. Beneficiaries are easy to make and change in your retirement accounts. You can do it online, by completing and mailing in a form that's provided by your trustee, or by directly contacting an authorized representative of the institution that administers your account.

You can make two types of beneficiary designations in a retirement account: primary and contingent. The most common primary designation is with couples where the partner or spouse is named as the primary beneficiary and the kids or other family members are listed as contingent beneficiaries. For example, if your spouse is named as the primary, then when you die he or she would inherit the balance in your account.

Usually, you cannot use a will or trust to leave certain kinds of assets, including:

- bank accounts for which you have named a pay-on-death beneficiary
- life insurance proceeds (they go to the beneficiary you named in the policy)
- stocks and bonds for which you have named a transfer-on-death beneficiary
- property owned as "community property with the right of survivorship," which automatically goes to the survivor when one of the co-owners dies
- property owned in joint tenancy, which automatically goes to the surviving spouse when you die
- individual retirement accounts, 401(k) plans, and certain pension funds, which go to the beneficiary you named in forms provided by the account custodian

If you created your will with the help of an attorney, he or she will make sure you have properly designated your beneficiaries using the correct wording. You need to include their full name, date of birth, and Social Security number. If your accounts are under the name of a trust, you include the name of the trust, the date you created it, and its tax identification number or your Social Security number.

Power of Attorney and Health Care Directives

A durable power of attorney ensures that someone you trust will be on hand to manage the many practical financial tasks that arise if you become incapacitated. For example, bills must be paid, bank deposits must be made, and someone must handle insurance and benefits paperwork. Many other matters may need attention as well, from property repairs to managing investments or a small business. In most cases, a durable power of attorney for finances is the best way to take care of tasks like these.

It's a good idea for everyone to have a durable power of attorney for finances in their estate plan. They're particularly important if you fear that health problems may make it impossible for you to handle your financial matters.

It's vitally important that those close to you understand the kind of medical treatment you would or would not want if you were unable to speak for yourself. The person you name can also make other necessary health care decisions for you if you are too ill or injured to direct your own care. Depending on where you live, you may get a durable power of attorney advance health care directive or a durable power of attorney for health care.

Estate Tax Considerations

Estate tax is not a concern for most people. The tax is levied on the property you own at your death, but a large amount of property is exempt from taxation. In 2009, that amount was $3.5 million, which means most people don't need to worry about estate tax. If you're married, estate tax won't be an issue until the second spouse dies. When the first spouse dies, everything left to the surviving spouse is tax free. If the second spouse owns all the property and it's worth more than the estate tax exemption, estate tax will be due. If that's the case, it's worth doing some advance tax planning.

For most families, probate is a waste of time and money. It typically takes from nine to eighteen months to file a deceased person's will with the court, gather the assets, pay debts, and eventually distribute what is left as the will directs. Fees for attorneys, appraisers, accountants, and probate court can reduce by about 5 percent the amount left for survivors to inherit. Unless relatives are fighting over who gets what or there are big claims against the estate, a court-supervised process is seldom necessary.

Applying What You've Learned

- ◆ Your estate plan is the final component in your retirement plan. It's your assurance that everything you have worked for all your life will be distributed to your loved ones according to your wishes.
- ◆ An estate plan arranges for the distribution of assets in your estate when you die or if you are incapacitated.
- ◆ Most estate plans begin with a will, which specifies who gets your property when you die. A will combined with a living trust will allow you to spell out what you want under specific circumstances.
- ◆ A will lets you name a personal guardian to raise your minor children if they are orphaned.
- ◆ Individual state laws determine whether a will or trust made by a resident is valid.
- ◆ Durable power of attorney is particularly important in the event that health problems make it impossible for you to handle your financial matters.

PART 4

PUTTING IT ALL TOGETHER

L et's put together your retirement plan—everything that you plan on doing before and after you retire. All of the notes and documentation that you've assembled about what's inside your 401(k), your investment options and financial goals, and your estate plan can be inserted into a binder so that it's at your fingertips when you need it. A well-coordinated retirement plan will assure that all of your retirement goals and objectives are met. To put the binder together, start by inserting dividers for the following sections:

♦ **401(k) Plan.** Here is where you keep documentation about what's in your 401(k) with detailed descriptions of your investment options and current monthly account statements. For tax reasons, keep all of the monthly (or quarterly) statements that you remove from the binder in a separate folder so that it doesn't become packed.

◆ **Savings Plan.** What you plan to save each month is documented in this section, showing where the money will come from and where it will be deposited. Include your monthly budget notes in this section. Your notes may include issues such as changing goals and priorities that were discussed in your monthly meetings with your partner.

◆ **Investment Plan.** Contributions you are making into your retirement accounts like your 401(k) and IRA are identified in this section, along with what you're investing in and how you're diversifying your assets.

◆ **Your Estate Plan.** Identify the steps you have taken or will take to develop your estate plan, such as creating a will or living trust and naming beneficiaries. Include in this section copies of insurance policies that protect you and your family.

When you are confident that you have assembled a complete retirement plan, have it reviewed by a knowledgeable friend or a professional, such as a CPA or certified financial planner. Any money you spend for this review is a small price to pay to assure that your plan is solid and tight. Include contingency actions in your retirement plan that you can take if certain assumptions that you've made don't work out. For example, what actions can you take if you are not able to meet your monthly living expenses? In fact, if you don't have lots of contingencies built into your plan, you probably don't have a solid plan.

Finally, give a copy of your estate plan or a complete copy of your retirement plan to a trusted family member or friend as a backup in case you misplace your copy.

CHAPTER 11

Applying Everything You've Learned

CONGRATULATIONS! YOU MADE it to the last chapter. You now know what you need to do to take control of your 401(k) plan and successfully manage it for the rest of your life. You've learned that smart investing is really a very simple process: focus on how you want your assets allocated in your 401(k) plan and concentrate on your goal of achieving market returns that meet your expectations.

There comes a point in every "how to make it" book like this one where readers are convinced they know where they've been and where they're going. And then when they turn the page, something unexpected happens that challenges all their assumptions. Well, that is where we are in this final chapter.

More Big Changes Are Out There

Let's take a journey back in time to make sure we all know where we've been. Go back to the early 1980s when the war on "stagflation" was won by Ronald Reagan and his political team. At the time, his screenwriter's script went something like this: a growing economy starts with low tax rates to leave people with more money to spend buying homes and investing in a risky stock market. All of these activities will assuredly serve to expand the economy without necessarily leading to higher inflation, interest, and tax rates. The screenwriter's thought at the time was that a healthy economy coupled with low-interest loans would prod Americans to spend aggressively to fuel even more growth. Throughout most of the 1980s, this formula seemed to work.

Continuing forward, investing in the 1990s and even the early 2000s was relatively simple. The economy and the stock market continued to grow rapidly, and the occasional recession or bear market didn't last long. Then, along came the "great recession" of 2008, bringing an end to the screenwriter's fantasyland script. Many of the economic megatrends that smoothed our walk down the yellow brick road disappeared.

Now, let's fast-forward to today. The trillions of dollars the United States is spending to recover from this recession will have long-lasting economic consequences for every American. For starters, it will fuel a rise in inflation, interest rates, and the taxes that will be required to pay for it all. Although investment diversification is now more critical than ever in your 401(k) to weather the pending economic storm, you'll also want to own a home and inflation-protected bonds.

If you own a stock fund that's headed for rough seas, be prepared to move quickly and sell it. Replace it with a promising winner like an index fund that you're prepared to monitor. However, if the ship starts to sink, there's no better ballast than cash to lessen your chances of going down with the ship. Overreacting to economic change is the last thing you'll want to do in these uncertain times.

The financial chaos that we find ourselves in today reveals just how much Americans were conned by the screenwriters, our political leaders. When our economy emerges from the current recession, the script will take on a decidedly different turn. As you leaf through the following pages, you'll see how the economy is poised to change and what the likely impact will be on your 401(k). Apply what you've learned from this book so that you can profit from the way it's going to be.

Know Where You've Been

America's retirement safety net is wearing thin. As 401(k) plans tanked, home prices also plummeted and jobs vanished. Millions of Americans went to sleep at the height of the recession thinking that at least one of their 401(k) investments would make it when they woke up. But the ongoing recession has shattered that dream. The safety net is about to give way to the legions of baby boomers who are starting to retire and will one day exhaust Social Security's financial surplus. The mounting trillions of dollars in government deficits will only compound the problem.

As my uncle Ben used to say, climbing out of the hole always takes a lot longer than falling in. If you do nothing, you will remain in the hole. Those that are willing to get up and start climbing will get out. How long that will take depends on three major factors: how quickly you can start living on what you make now or later, how much you can save, and how aggressive you are at managing your 401(k) investments.

Know every option that's in your 401(k) plan if you want to save it. You've got to know by name each of the investment options that are available to you and how they have performed over the last three years. Your plan's provider can make that information available to you and often provides online access to your investment options as well.

The beginning chapters of the book address the importance of living within your means. You're now going to have to walk the walk. You have no choice but to cut your spending back to what you can afford before you retire and stop living from payday to payday. Start by burning your credit cards and ignoring the spendthrifts who are continuing on their hapless way to financial destruction. Make a vow to yourself that you're not going to join them.

Know Where You're Going

If you want to get to your destination, then you've got to know where you're going. And you do if you put your 401(k) plan through the "retirement readiness test" that was covered in the beginning of this book. You should now know how much you'll need to retire on and how much you'll need to save to meet your needs. That task should be less daunting if you use some of the excellent help tools available online.

One of the major benefits of using online retirement calculators is that they give you a reality check on the investment you're making in your 401(k). Will the amount you're saving enable you to accumulate what you'll need for retirement? A good calculator can help you answer that question and identify any shortfalls in your retirement plan. Do you need to increase your contributions, adjust your investment to achieve a higher rate of return, or do a combination of both?

Know How to Get There

Whether or not the recession has hit you directly, now is the time to look at ways to save everything you can for your retirement. Be aware of what you can do right now to find the additional money you may need to supplement your 401(k) plan. Deposit into a savings account all extra money that you have every week. That's one way to keep yourself from spending it on something else you don't need, and you'll be richer for saving it.

Although there's some art and science involved in picking investment winners, it's easier if you approach your selection of funds rationally. If you're tired of paying the high expenses charged by mutual funds and being burned by the industry's dismal returns, then invest in low-cost index funds. Remember, an index fund is a fixed market basket of stocks, bonds, and other securities that will track a benchmark. Index funds have several advantages over traditional funds in that they're typically cheaper to own and easier to buy or sell than traditional mutual funds. Most trade just like a stock on the exchanges.

No one likes to lose money in their investment, especially if it's more than they can afford. The amount of risk you're willing to take may depend on how soon you'll need the money—your time horizon to retire. If you are nearing retirement, then this is the time when you need to move your money out of high-risk investments into low-risk investments such as certificates of deposit and bond funds to protect your retirement dollars.

Know What to Do When You Get There

Figuring out how to withdraw a secure retirement income from a portfolio is a challenge in the best of times. If you're thinking about retiring in the near future, will you be able to invest your money wisely so that it will continue to grow? Are you ready to retire now? Can you afford it, and will the money last a lifetime? An important part of protecting your retirement accounts is to set aside enough money to take care of unplanned expenses. Even if retirement is your primary financial goal, putting all of your money into a 401(k) or IRA is not the best way to reach that goal. Keep some cash on hand to protect yourself against the unexpected.

Having been through the worst recession since the Great Depression, be careful you don't go into a loss-avoidance mode. If you avoid all market risk, you'll be vulnerable to inflation and you'll risk outliving your money. Hiding in cash probably won't see you through your retirement years. No one investment can protect you from every risk you'll face, so have a market basket of stable investments that together will provide an income you're not likely to outlive.

In addition, don't let yourself get caught in the trap of thinking that you are diversifying just because you've got a stock fund that has been performing well over several years. That won't help if the entire market takes a nosedive. Even if you've assembled a portfolio of good solid performers, you're still at the mercy of an economic downturn, so watch all of your investments closely. Be ready, willing, and able to change your investment mix if the times warrant it.

If you need the extra money when you retire, there's no use in trying to avoid the inevitable. So get ahead of the curve and start thinking like an entrepreneur. If you need to supplement your retirement income, be prepared to take whatever appropriate action you can to solve the problem.

The needs of your family are still there at any stage in your life. There are special tax benefits within your retirement accounts that can be extended to your family. Estate planning can also offer tax benefits. Making a will and living trust is not difficult, but it is undeniably a serious and sobering process. Make sure you have an estate plan that arranges for the distribution of your assets when you die or if you become incapacitated.

Have a Good Journey

Envision a board game, like the game of Life. The game really started with your first paycheck and took off from there. In reality your retirement plan is your trip plan in the game. It's the road map that shows you where you've been and where you need to go to reach your final destination, a beautiful oasis called retirement. All of the notes and documentation that you've assembled along the way will fit snugly in a travel binder so that everything is at your fingertips. If you get lost or need help navigating through tough economic times, refer to your road map for directions. It can be your compass and a reliable guide as you head into the future.

I want to take this opportunity to wish you and your family the very best of luck and success as you venture down the road to retirement.

Glossary

Active management: *An investment style that presumes that investments guided by the manager of a fund with market and economic insight will perform better than investments that are not actively managed*

Adjusted gross income (AGI): *The amount of income that's calculated by adding an individual's work income and other sources of income*

Asset allocation: *The different percentages of assets invested in a portfolio, e.g., 50 percent equities, 25 percent bonds, and 25 percent cash*

Capital gains tax rate: *The percentage of profits made from investing that must be paid in taxes*

Certificate of deposit: *A bank's promissory note to repay the amount deposited with interest at a future date*

Compound interest: *Interest paid on the principal and also on the accumulated interest that has been earned by the principal*

Contributions: *The amount of cash or other assets deposited in a retirement account*

Defined benefit plan: *A retirement plan that pays a specific retirement benefit once an employee meets a certain requirement, such as years of service*

Defined contribution plan: *A retirement plan with specific rules that dictate when and who can make deposits for specified amounts*

Direct rollover: *A process that directly transfers assets from one retirement plan into another*

Dollar cost averaging: *A savings strategy involving investing the same dollar amount at fixed intervals so if share prices increase, fewer shares are bought; if they decrease, more shares are bought at different intervals*

Exchange traded funds (ETFs): *Pooled investment accounts that, like mutual funds, hold a basket of many individual investments and are traded on the stock exchanges*

Fixed annuity: *A tax-deferred financial instrument marketed by insurance companies and brokerage firms that pays a fixed rate of interest that readjusts annually*

Individual retirement accounts (IRAs): *Tax-deferred retirement plans*

Matching contribution: *When an employer promises to match a certain percentage, within limits, on an employee's contribution into his or her retirement plan*

Money market fund: *An investment account in which the cash in the account is accessible at any time*

Mutual funds: *A combination of multiple investments like stocks and bonds bundled together into one investment product*

Passive management: *An investment management style that seeks to match the market's performance*

Plan provider: *The company hired by an employer to administer its retirement plan, often acting as the plan's trustee as well*

Pretax contribution: *A tax-deferred retirement amount that a person is permitted to deduct from his or her tax obligation*

Prime rate: *The interest rate banks charge preferred customers*

Profit-sharing contribution: *An employer's contribution made to its employees' retirement accounts that is based on company profits*

Rebalancing: *The process of adjusting the allocation of assets in a retirement plan that correct for different assets having performed differently over time*

Roth IRA: *An individual retirement account in which taxes do not accrue when funds are withdrawn*

Sixty-day rollover: *The grace period allowed to transfer assets from one tax-deferred retirement account into another tax-deferred retirement account without incurring an early withdrawal penalty*

Summary Plan Description (SPD): *A rule book that governs a specific 401(k) plan, available from the plan's provider or the employer*

Target date fund: *A mutual fund whose allocation of assets are tailored to perform best within a time frame for a specific event, like your retirement date*

Tax deferred: *The income gains generated by investments that do not become taxable until the funds are withdrawn from the account*

Taxable income: *The earnings from an individual's job and investments that are taxable each year*

Timing the market: *Determining at a particular moment in time which way the market is going—up, down, or sideways*

Trustee fees: *The costs paid by investors in retirement accounts that can include sales commissions, management, and administration fees*

Variable annuities: *Annuities that change in value based on the performance of subaccounts made up of a market basket of individual stock and bond investments*

Online Resources

Budgeting

fidelity.com/myplan
flexibleretirementplanner.com
money.com
personalbudgeting.com
simpleplanning.com
smartmoney.com
tdameritrade.com

Calculators—Retirement and Risk

calcxml.com
choosetosave.org/calculators
dinkytown.com
fincalc.com
kiplinger.com
riskgrades.com

schwab.com
socialsecurity.gov/estimator
troweprice.com/ric

Credit Cards and Credit Scores

annualcreditreport.com
cardratings.com
myfico.com

Debt Avoidance

bankrupcyinfo.com
cgi.money.cnn.com
clearbankruptcy.com
debtorsanonymous.org
defeatthedebt.com
money.com
simpleliving.net
smartmoney.com

Estate Planning

financialengines.com
impower.com

kiplinger.com
money.com
morningstar.com
nolo.com
quicken.com
smartmoney.com/retirement

Financial Information and News Sites

businessweek.com
fidelity.com
investools.com
kiplinger.com
money.cnn.com
morningstar.com
quicken.com
simpleplanning.com
smartinvestmentbook.com
yodlee.com

Professional Advice

aicpa.org
fpanet.org
napfa.org

Real Estate

bankrate.com
craigslist.com
realestate.msn.com
wheretoretire.com

Reducing Expenses

billshrink.com
campusbookrentals.com
carpoolworld.com
chegg.com
energystar.gov
erideshare.com

Retirement Planning

flexibleretirementplanner.com
immediateannuities.com
kiplinger.com
money.com
quicken.com/retirement/planner
schwab.com
smartmoney.com

Reverse Mortgages

aarp.com
revmort.com/nrmla

Shopping Online

bluefly.com
craigslist.com
ebay.com
yoox.com

Social Security and Medicare

medicare.gov
socialsecurity.gov
socialsecurity.gov/estimator

Stock Charts and Market Timing

stockcharts.com
vectorvest.com

Stocks, Mutual Funds, Index Funds, and Bond Funds

fidelity.com
fundalarm.com
schwab.com
timingthemarket.net
troweprice.com
vanguard.com

Tax Information

completetax.com
irs.gov

Index

About the Author

DAVID RYE was the founder of Computech Corporation and, later, a director of IBM. He earned an MBA with honors from Seattle University. He is currently president of Western Publications, publishing personal finance books from his Scottsdale, Arizona, office. David's award-winning books include *The Corporate Game*, *Stop Managing and Lead*, *Starting Up*, and *1001 Ways to Inspire Yourself*. He's also a consultant, showing managers how to inspire their employees to get the most out of their 401(k) plans. David invites you to visit his website at Itsboomtimebaby.com.